MOBILE COMPUTING AND WIRELESS COMMUNICATION

MCWC

DR. ADITI SHARMA

This book is dedicated to my Friends and my dear studnets, For upgrade knowlage.

Contents

Preface

This book offers guidelines on how mobile computing services can be used in order to simplify the mobile users'. The main contribution of this book is enhancing mobile computing and application development stages as analysis, design, development and test.

1

Introduction:- Transmission Fundamentals, Communication, Protocol and TCP/IP Suite

◦❦◦

Introduction of Mobile computing

- **Mobile Computing** is a technology that allows transmission of data, voice, and video via a computer or any other wireless-enabled device.
- It can be defined as a computing environment of physical mobility.
- A mobile computing system allows a user to perform a task from anywhere while on move.

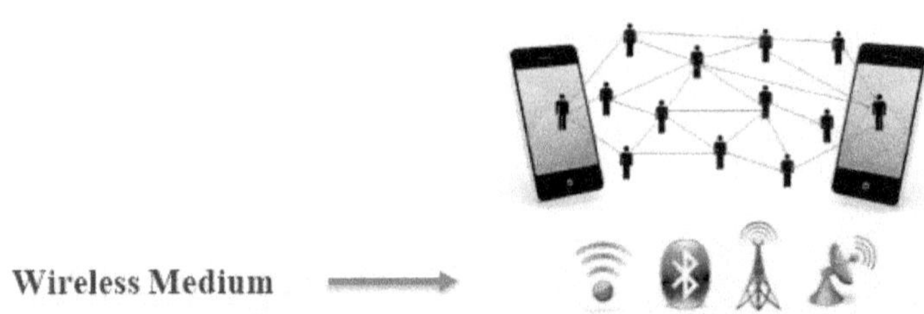

Figure 1: Mobile Computing

- Mobile Computing involves the following:

  - Mbile cmmunication

    - Mobile communication refers to the infrastructure put in place to ensure that seamless and reliable communication.
    - These would include devices such as protocols, services, bandwidth, and portals necessary to facilitate and support the stated services.
    - Media is unguided/wireless; the infrastructure is basically radio wave-oriented.

  - Mbile Hardware

    - Mobile hardware includes mobile devices or device components that receive or access the service of mobility.
    - Devices are laptops, smartphones, tablet Pc's, Personal Digital Assistants.
    - These devices have capable of sending and receiving signals.
    - These devices are configured to operate in full- duplex means sending and receiving signals at the same time in wireless network.

- ○ Mbile Sftware

  - Mobile software is the actual program that runs on the mobile hardware.
  - In other terms, it is the operating system of the appliance.
  - It's the essential component that operates the mobile device.
  - It deals with the characteristics and requirements of mobile applications.

  - **For example**, the manufacturers of Apple's iPhone OS, Google's Android' Microsoft Windows Mobile, Research In Motion's Blackberry OS.

- *Attribute of Mobility*
- User Mobility

  - ○ User should be able to move from one physical location to another location and use the same service.
  - ○ **Example**: User moves from London to New York and uses the Internet in either place to access the corporate application.

- Network Mobility

  - ○ User should be able to move from one network to another network and use the same service.
  - ○ **Example**: User moves from Hong Kong to Singapore and uses the same GSM phone to access the corporate application.

- Bearer Mobility

  - ○ User should be able to move from one bearer to another while using the same service.
  - ○ **Example**: User is unable to access the WAP bearer due to some problem in the GSM network then he should be able

to use voice or SMS bearer to access that same corporate application.
- ○ Like Hike Messenger

- Device Mobility

  - ○ User should be able to move from one device to another and use the same service.
  - ○ **Example**: User is using a PC to do his work. During the day, while he is on the street he would like to use his mobile to access the corporate application.

- Session Mobility

  - ○ A user session should be able to move from one user - agent environment to another.
  - ○ **Example**: An unfinished session moving from a mobile device to a desktop computer is a good example.

- Service Mobility

  - ○ User should be able to move from one service to another.
  - ○ **Example**: User is writing a mail. Suddenly, he needs to refer to something else. In a PC, user simply opens another service and moves between them. User should be able to do the same in small wireless devices.

- *Limitation of Mobile Computing*
- Limitations of the wireless network

  - ○ Heterogeneity of fragmented networks
  - ○ Frequent disconnections
  - ○ Limited communication bandwidth

- Limitations imposed by mobility

- ○ Lack of mobility awareness by system / applications
- ○ Route breakages

- Limitations of the mobile computer

  - ○ Short battery lifetime
  - ○ Limited capacities (memory, processing speed, etc.)

- *Introduction of Wireless Communication*
- **Wireless Communication** involves the transmission of information over a distance without the help of wires, cables or any other forms of electrical conductors.
- It is a term that connecting and communicating between two or more devices using a wireless signal through wireless communication technologies and devices.
-

- Host Mobility

  - ○ User should be able to move while the device is a host computer.
  - ○ **Example**: The laptop computer of a user is a host for grid computing network. It is connected to a LAN port. Suddenly, the user realizes that he needs to leave for an offsite meeting. He disconnects from the LAN and should get connected to wireless LAN while his laptop being the host for grid
-   computing network.

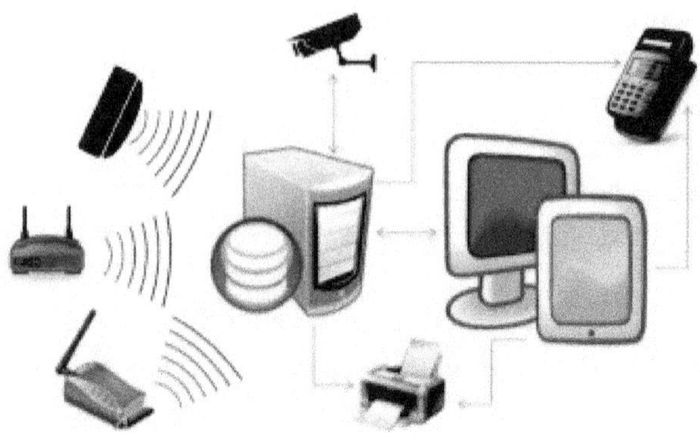

Figure 2: Wireless Communication

- The transmitted distance can be anywhere between a few meters (**for example:** a television's remote control) and thousands of kilometers (**for example:** radio communication).
- Wireless communication can be used for cellular telephony, wireless access to the internet, wireless home networking, and so on.
- *Applications of Wireless Communication*
- GPS Units
- Wireless keyboard-mouse
- Headsets
- Radio Receivers
- Satellite Television
- Broadcast Television
- Cordless Telephones etc...
- *Signals - Basics*
- A signal is an electrical or electromagnetic current that is used for carrying data from one device or network to another.
- It is the key component behind virtually all:

- Communication
- Computing
- Networking
- Electronic devices

- A signal can be either analog or digital.
- Here, we are concerned with electromagnetic signals used as a means to transmit information.
- An electromagnetic signal is a function of time, but it can also be expressed as a function of frequency; that is, the signal consists of components of different frequencies.

  - Time Domain
  - Frequency Domain

- The frequency domain view of a signal is far more important to an understanding of data transmission than a time domain view.
- As a function of time, an electromagnetic signal can be either analog or digital.
- **An analog signal** is one in which the signal intensity varies in a smooth fashion over time.
- In other words, there are no breaks or discontinuities in the signal.
- **A digital signal** is one in which the signal intensity maintains a constant level for some period of time and then changes to another constant level.

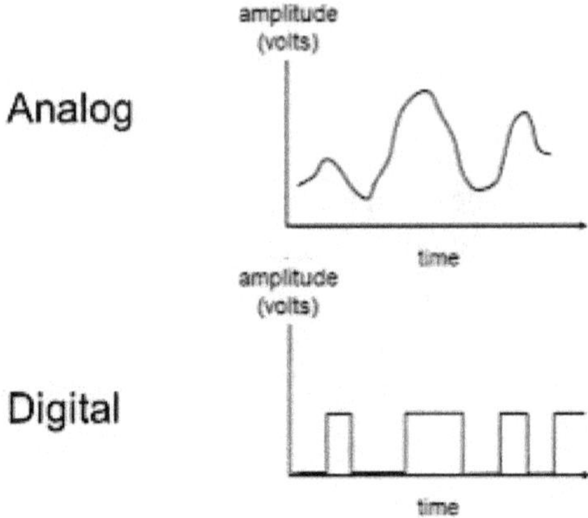

Figure 3: Analog and Digital Waveforms

- Figure shows **examples** of both kinds of signals. The analog signal might represent speech, and the digital signal might represent binary 1s and 0s.
- **Periodic signal**: An analog or digital signal pattern that repeats over time.
- **Aperiodic signal**: An analog or digital signal pattern that doesn't
- repeat over time.

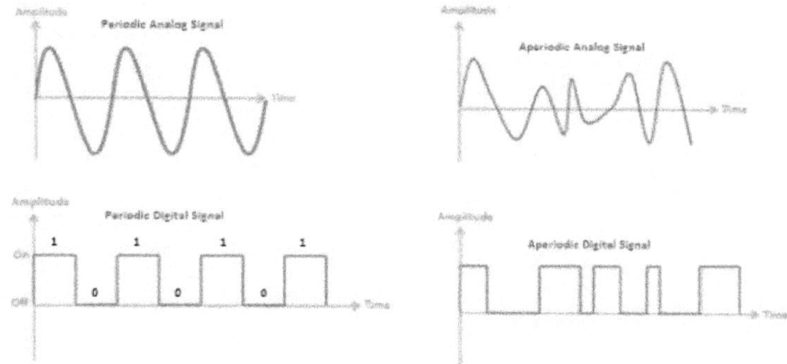

Figure 4: Periodic and Aperiodic Signal

- **Peak amplitude (A):** Maximum value or strength of the signal over time. Typically measured in volts.
- **Frequency (f):** Rate, in cycles per second, or Hertz (Hz), at which the signal repeats.
- **Phase (?):** A measurement of the relative position in time within a single period of a signal.
- **Wavelength (?):** A distance occupied by a single cycle of the signal.

  - **Example:** Speed of light is $v = 3x108$ m/s. Wavelength is $?f = v$ (or $? = vT$)

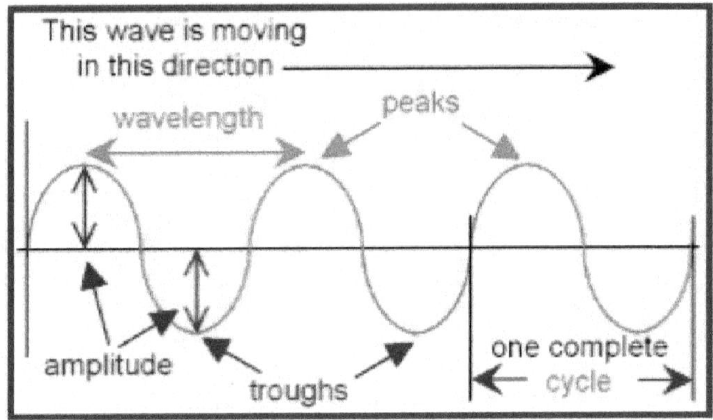

Figure 5: Different terms of waveform

Analog and Digital Data Transmission

- The terms analog and digital correspond, roughly, to continuous and discrete, respectively.
- These two terms are used frequently in data communications in at least three contexts:

  - Data

  - Signals
  - Transmission

- We define data as entities that convey meaning, or information.
- Signals are electric or electromagnetic representations of data.
- Transmission is the communication of data by the propagation and processing of signals.
- **Analog data** take on continuous values in some interval.

  - **For example**, voice and video are continuously varying patterns of intensity.

- ○ Most data collected by sensors, such as temperature and pressure, are continuous valued.

- **Digital data** take on discrete values.

  - ○ **Examples** are text and integers.

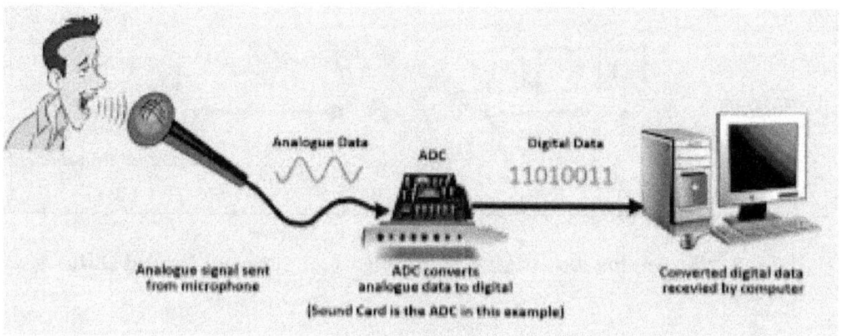

Figure 6: Analog and Digital Data

- **An analog signal** is a continuously varying electromagnetic wave that may be propagated over a variety of media, depending on frequency.

  - ○ **Examples** are copper wire media, such as twisted pair and coaxial cable; fiber optic cable; and atmosphere or space propagation (wireless).

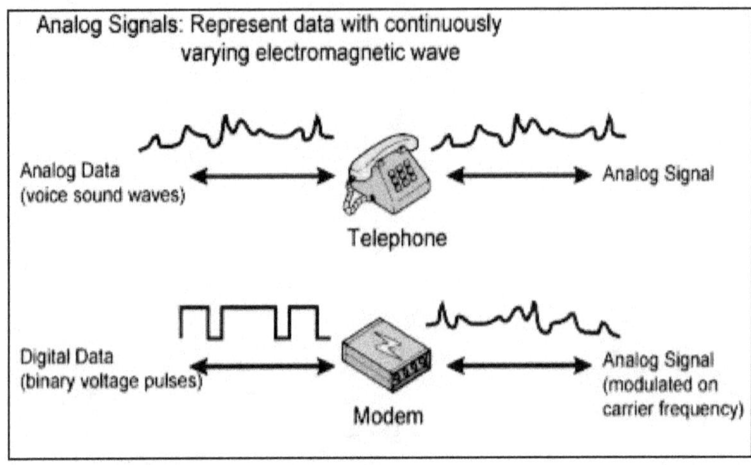

Figure 7: Analog and Digital Signaling of Analog and Digital Data

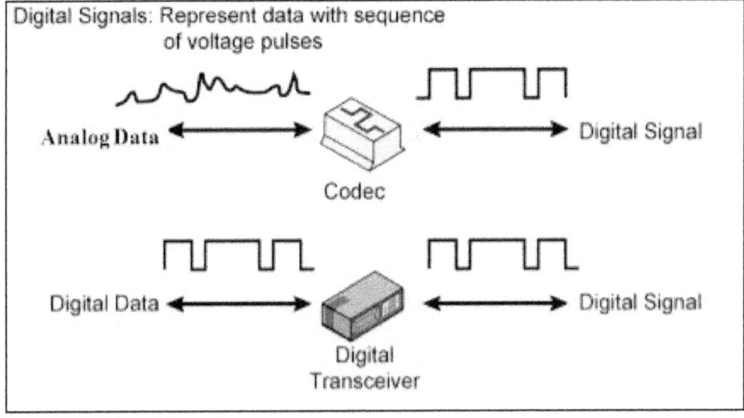

Figure 8: Analog and Digital Signaling of Analog and Digital Data

- **A digital signal** is a sequence of voltage pulses that may be transmitted over a copper wire medium.
- **Example**, a constant positive voltage level may represent binary 0 and a constant negative voltage level may represent binary 1.
- The principal advantages of digital signaling are that it is generally cheaper than analog signaling and is less susceptible to noise interference.
- The principal disadvantage is that digital signals suffer more from attenuation than do analog signals.
- **In frequency domain view**, A signals lie in the frequency range, theoretically signals are composed of many sinusoidal signals with different frequencies (like Fourier Series).
- It is actually composed of infinite sinusoidal signal at different amplitudes, frequencies, and phases. An electromagnetic signal can be made up of **many frequencies.**

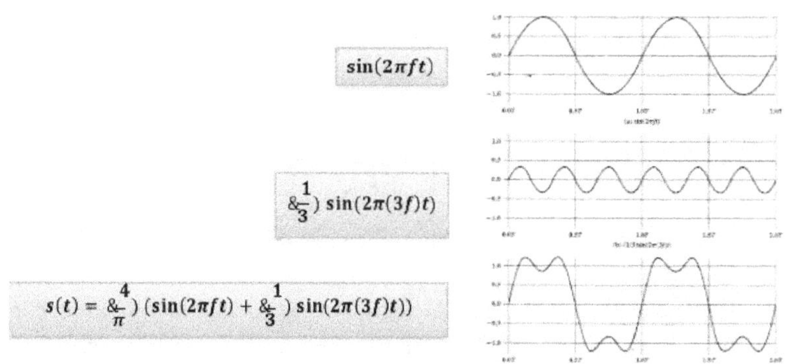

Figure 9: Frequency Domain View

- *Channel Capacity*
- The maximum rate at which data can be transmitted over a given communication path, or channel, under given conditions is referred to as the channel capacity.

- There are four concepts here that we are trying to relate to one another:
- *Shannon and Nyquist Capacity Formula*
- Two theoretical formulas were developed to calculate the data rate:
- **Nyquist** for a noiseless channel
- **Shannon** for a noisy channel
- Data rate governs the speed of data transmission.
- A very important consideration in data communication is how fast we can send data, in bits per second, over a channel.
-
- **Data rate**: This is the rate, in bits per second (bps), at which data can be communicated.
- Data rate depends upon 3 factors:

  1. The bandwidth available
  2. Number of levels in digital signal
  3. The quality of the channel – level of noise

- **Bandwidth**: This is the bandwidth of the transmitted signal as constrained by the transmitter and the nature of the transmission medium, expressed in cycles per second, or Hertz.
- **Noise**: We are concerned with the average level of noise over the communications path.
- **Error rate**: This is the rate at which errors occur, where an error is the reception of a 1 when a 0 was transmitted or the reception of a 0 when a 1 was transmitted.

Noiseless Channel : Nyquist Bit Rate
C = ? ? ???? ?
For a noiseless channel, the Nyquist bit rate formula defines the theoretical maximum bit rate.

- Where:

- ○ B is the bandwidth of the channel
- ○ M is the number of signal levels used to represent data
- ○ C is the bit rate in bits per second.

- Bandwidth is a fixed quantity, so it cannot be changed. Hence, the data rate is directly proportional to the number of signal levels.
- Note that, Increasing the levels of a signal may reduce the reliability of the system.
- **Example-1**: Consider a noiseless channel with a bandwidth of 4000 Hz transmitting a signal with two signal levels. What can be the maximum bit rate?
- **Answer**: Bit-Rate = 2 * 4000 * log2(2) = 8000bps
- **Example**-2: We need to send 250 kbps over a noiseless channel with a bandwidth of 30 kHz. How many signal levels do we need?
- **Answer**: 250000 = 2 * 30000 * log2(L)
- log2(L) = 4.17
- L = 2^4.17 = 18 levels
- Noisy Channel : Shannon Capacity
- In reality, we cannot have a noiseless channel; the channel is always noisy.
- $C = ? ???(? + ???)$

Shannon capacity is used to determine the theoretical highest
- data rate for a noisy channel.
- Where:

- ○ B is the bandwidth of the channel
- ○ SNR is the signal-to-noise ratio
- ○ C is the capacity of the channel in bits per second

- Bandwidth is a fixed quantity, so it cannot be changed.
- So, the channel capacity is directly proportional to the power of the signal, as SNR = Power of signal / power of noise.
- The signal-to-noise ratio (S/N) is usually expressed in decibels (dB).

- **Example**: A telephone line normally has a bandwidth of 3000 Hz (300 to 3300 Hz) assigned for data communication. The SNR is usually 3162. What will be the capacity for this channel?
- **Answer**: C = 3000 * log2(1 + SNR) = 3000 * 11.62 = 34860 bps
- *Transmission Media*

    A transmission medium can be defined as anything that can carry information from a source to a destination.
- Guided transmission media
- Unguided transmission media

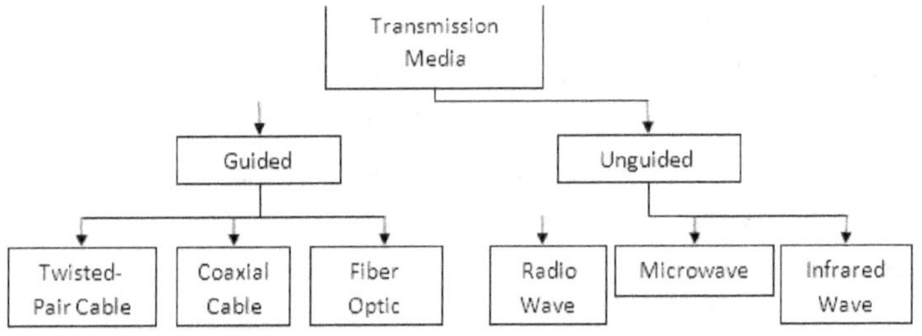

Figure 10: Classification Transmission Media

Guided Transmission Media

A.   Magnetic media B. Twisted pair

C. Coaxial cable D. Fiber optics

- Guided media, which are those that provide a channel from one device to another, include twisted-pair cable, coaxial cable, and fiber-optic cable.
- A signal travelling along any of these media is directed and contained by the physical limit of the medium.

A.   Magnetic Media

- One of the most common ways to transport data from one computer to another is to write them onto magnetic tape or removable media (e.g., recordable DVDs), physically transport the tape or disks to the destination machine, and read them back in again.
- Although this method is not as sophisticated as using a geosynchronous communication satellite, it is often more cost effective, especially for applications in which high bandwidth or cost per bit transported is the key factor.

B. Twisted Pair

- A twisted pair consists of two insulated copper wires, typically about 1 mm thick.
- The wires are twisted together in a helical form, just like a DNA molecule.
- Twisting is done because two parallel wires constitute a fine antenna.
- When the wires are twisted, the waves from different twists cancel out, so the wire radiates less effectively.

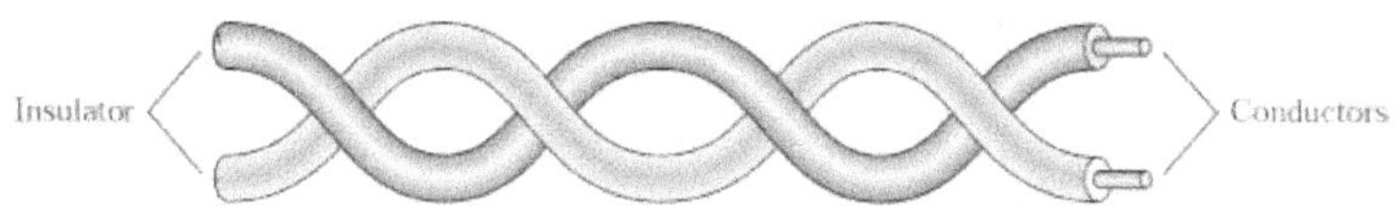

Figure 11: Twisted Pair Cable

Why cable is twisted?

- If the two wires are parallel, the effect of these unwanted signals is not the same in both wires because they are at different locations relatives to the noise or crosstalk sources.
- This results in a difference at the receiver.

- By twisting the pair, a balance is maintained.

Types of Twisted-Pair Cable

1. Unshielded twisted-pair (UTP)

- Twisted pair cabling comes in several varieties, two of which are important for computer networks.
- **Category 3** twisted pairs consist of two insulated wires gently twisted together.
- **Category 5** is the more advanced twisted pairs were introduced.
- They are similar to category 3 pairs, but with more twists per centimeter, which results in less crosstalk and a better-quality signal over longer distances, making them more suitable for high-speed computer communication.
- Latest categories are 6 and 7, which are capable of handling signals with bandwidths of 250 MHz and 600 MHz, respectively (versus a mere 16 MHz and 100 MHz for categories 3 and 5, respectively).

Category 3 UTP.   **Category 5 UTP.**

Figure 12: Unshielded twisted-pair

2) Shielded twisted-pair (STP)

- STP cable has a metal foil or braided mesh covering that encases each pair of insulated conductors.
- Metal casing improves the quality of cable by preventing the penetration of noise or crosstalk.

- It is bulkier and more expensive.
- Applications:

  ○ Used in telephone lines to provide voice and data channels.
  ○ The DSL lines uses by telephone companies use the high-bandwidth capability of UTP cables.
  ○ LANs, such as 10Base-T, 100Base-T, also uses twisted-pair cables.

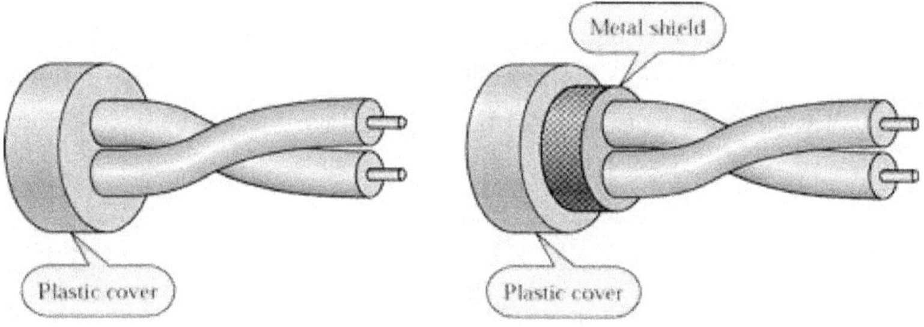

Figure 13: UTP and STP Cable

A. Coaxial Cable

- It has better shielding than twisted pairs, so it can span longer distances at higher speeds.
- Two kinds of coaxial cable are widely used. One kind, 50-ohm cable, is commonly used when it is intended for digital transmission from the start.
- The other kind, 75-ohm cable, is commonly used for analog transmission and cable television but is becoming more important with the advent of Internet over cable.
- A coaxial cable consists of a stiff copper wire as the core, surrounded by an insulating material.

- The insulator is encased by a cylindrical conductor, often as a closely-woven braided mesh.
- The outer conductor is covered in a protective plastic sheath.
- The construction and shielding of the coaxial cable give it a good combination of high bandwidth and excellent noise immunity.

- The bandwidth possible depends on the cable quality, length, and signal-to-noise ratio of the data signal. Modern cables have a bandwidth of close to 1 GHz.
- Coaxial cables used to be widely used within the telephone system for long-distance lines but have now largely been replaced by fiber optics on long-haul routes.

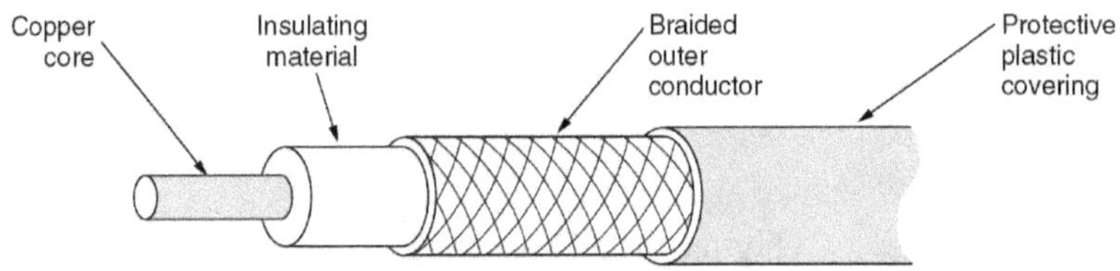

Figure 14: Coaxial Cable

C. Fiber Optics

- A fiber-optic cable is made of glass or plastic and transmits signals in the form of light.
- Optical fibers use reflection to guide light through a channel.
- A glass or plastic core is surrounded by a cladding of less dense glass or plastic.
- The difference in density of the two materials must be such that a beam of light moving through a core is reflected off the cladding instead of being refracted into it.

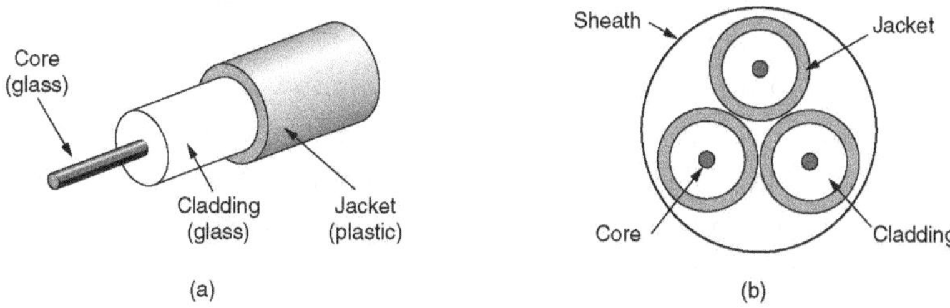

Figure 15: Fiber Optic Cable

Fiber optic cables are similar to coax, except without the braid.

- Figure shows a single fiber viewed from the side. At the center is the glass core through which the light propagates.
- The core is surrounded by a glass cladding with a lower index of refraction than the core, to keep all the light in the core.
- Next comes a thin plastic jacket to protect the cladding. Fibers are typically grouped in bundles, protected by an outer sheath. Figure shows a sheath with three fibers.

Unguided (Wireless) transmission media

A. Radio Transmission
B. Microwave Transmission
C. Infrared
D. Light wave Transmission

- Unguided media transport electromagnetic waves without using a physical conductor. This type of communication is often referred to as wireless communication.

A. Radio Transmission

- Radio waves are easy to generate, can travel long distances, and can penetrate buildings easily, so they are widely used for communication, both indoors and outdoors.
- Radio waves also are omnidirectional, meaning that they travel in all directions from the source, so the transmitter and receiver do not have to be carefully aligned physically.
- The properties of radio waves are frequency dependent.
- At low frequencies, radio waves pass through obstacles well, but the power falls off sharply with distance from the source, roughly as 1/r2 in air.
- At high frequencies, radio waves tend to travel in straight lines and bounce off obstacles. They are also absorbed by rain.
- At all frequencies, radio waves are subject to interference from motors and other electrical equipment.

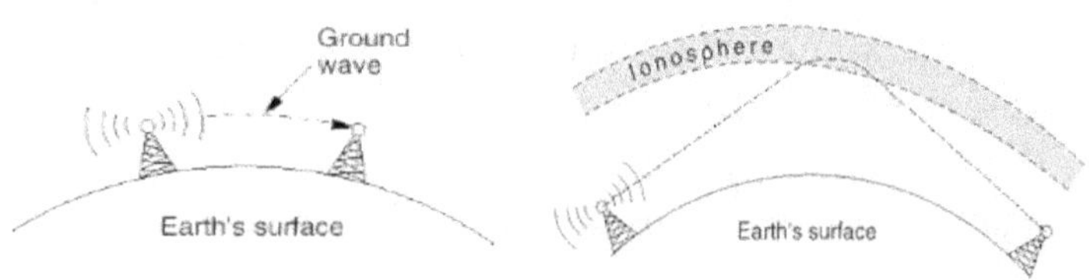

- In the VLF, LF, and MF bands, radio waves follow the curvature of the earth.
- In the HF they bounce off the ionosphere

B. Microwave Transmission

- Since the microwaves travel in a straight line, if the towers are too far apart, the earth will get in the way .Consequently, repeaters are needed periodically.

- Unlike radio waves at lower frequencies, microwaves do not pass through buildings well. In addition, even though the beam may be well focused at the transmitter, there is still some divergence in space.
- Above 100 MHz, the waves **travel in straight lines** and can therefore be narrowly focused. Concentrating all the energy into a small beam using a **parabolic antenna** gives a much higher signal to noise ratio.
- Advantages:

  - No right way is needed (compared to wired media).
  - Relatively inexpensive.
  - Simple to install.

- Disadvantages:

  - Do not pass through buildings well.
  - Multipath fading problem (the delayed waves cancel the signal).
  - Absorption by rain above 8 GHz.
  - Severe shortage of spectrum.

C. Infrared

- Unguided infrared and millimeter waves are widely used for short-range communication.
- The remote controls used on televisions, VCRs, and stereos all use infrared communication.
- They are relatively directional, cheap, and easy to build but have a major drawback: they do not pass through solid objects (try standing between your remote control and your television and see if it still works).
- In general, as we go from long-wave radio toward visible light, the waves behave more and more like light and less and less like radio.

- On the other hand, the fact that infrared waves do not pass through solid walls well is also a plus.
- It means that an infrared system in one room of a building will not interfere with a similar system in adjacent rooms or buildings.
- Furthermore, security of infrared systems against eavesdropping is better than that of radio systems precisely for this reason.
- Therefore, no government license is needed to operate an infrared system, in contrast to radio systems, which must be licensed outside the ISM bands.

Communication Network

- Communication networks can be categories by their size as well as their purpose.
- The size of a network can be expressed by the geographic area.
- Some of the different networks based on size are:

  - LAN – Local Area Network
  - MAN – Metropolitan Area Network
  - WAN – Wide Area Network

LAN (Local Area Network)

- It is privately-owned networks within a single building or campus of up to a few kilometers in size.
- They are widely used to connect personal computers and workstations in company offices and factories to share resources (e.g., printers) and exchange information.
- LANs are easy to design and troubleshoot
- In LAN, all the machines are connected to a single cable.
- Different types of topologies such as Bus, Ring, Star, and Tree are used.

- The data rates for LAN range from 4 to 16 Mbps.
- They transfer data at high speeds (higher bandwidth).
- They exist in a limited geographical area.
- Connectivity and resources, especially the transmission media, usually are managed by the company which running the LAN.

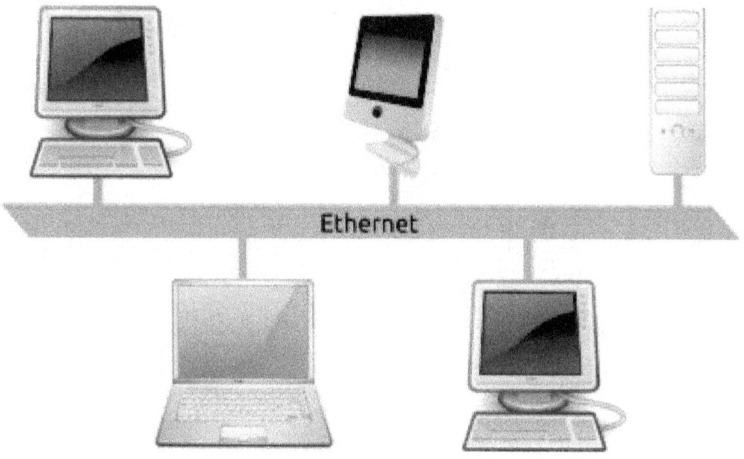

Figure 16: Local Area Network

MAN (Metropolitan Area Network)

- A metropolitan area network, or MAN, covers a city. The best-known example of a MAN is the cable television network available in many cities.
- A MAN is basically a bigger version of a LAN and normally uses similar technology.
- At first, the companies began jumping into the business, getting contracts from city governments to wire up an entire

city.
- The next step was television programming and even entire channels designed for cable only. Often these channels were highly specialized, such as all news, all sports, all cooking, and so on.

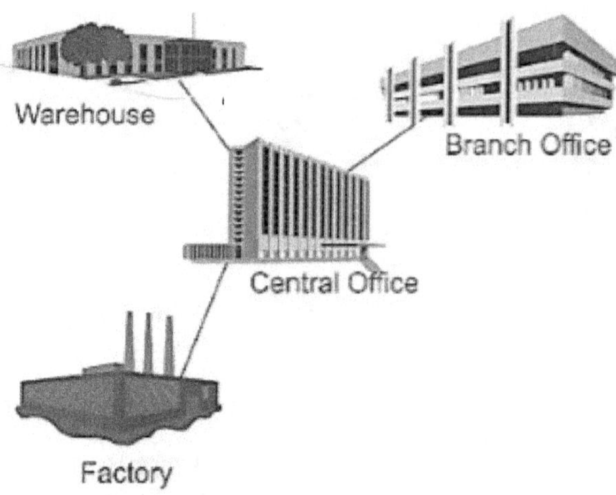

Figure 17: Metropolitan Area Network

WAN (Wide Area Network)

- WAN, spans a large geographical area, often a country or continent.
- It contains a collection of machines intended for running user (i.e., application) programs. We will follow traditional usage and call these machines hosts.
- The hosts are connected by a communication subnet, or just subnet for short.
- In most wide area networks, the subnet consists of two distinct components: transmission lines and switching

elements. Transmission lines move bits between machines.

- The communication between different users of WAN is established using leased telephone lines or satellite links and similar channels.

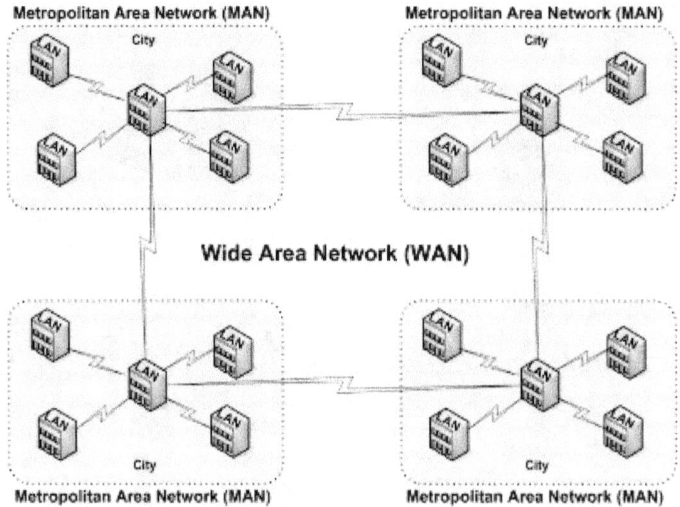

Figure 18: Wide Area Network

What Is the Internet?

- The Internet is a computer network that interconnects hundreds of millions of computing devices throughout the world.
- When two computers are connected over the Internet, they can send and receive all kinds of information such as text, graphics, voice, video, and computer programs.

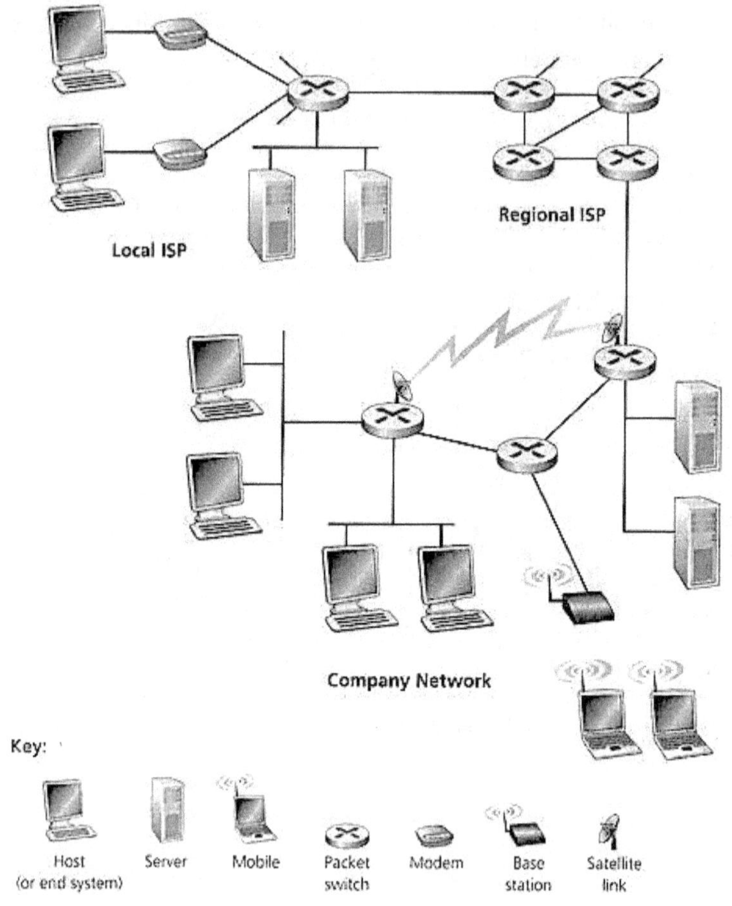

Figure 19: Some pieces of the Internet

Switching Techniques

- For transmission of data beyond a local area, communication is typically achieved by transmitting data from source to destination through a network of intermediate switching nodes; this switched network design is sometimes used to implement

LANs and MANs as well.
- Switching Techniques - In large networks there might be multiple paths linking sender and receiver. Information may be switched as it travels through various communication channels.

Circuit Switching

- Circuit switching is used in public telephone networks and is the basis for private networks built on leased-lines.
- Circuit switching was developed to handle voice traffic but also digital data (although inefficient)
- With circuit switching a dedicated path is established between two stations for communication.
- Switching and transmission resources within the network are reserved for the exclusive use of the circuit for the duration of the connection.

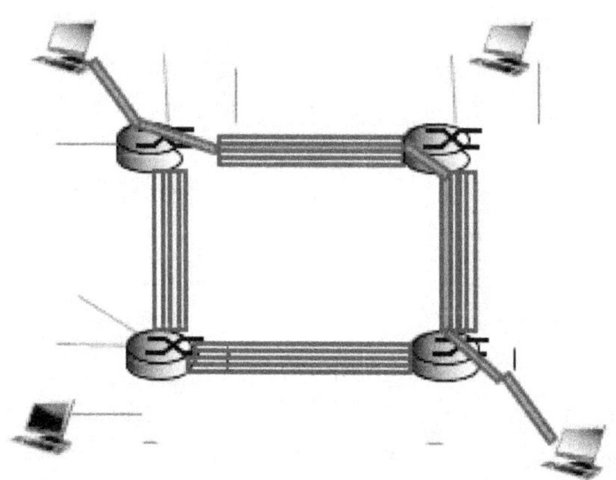

Figure 20: Circuit Switching Network

- The connection is transparent: once it is established, it appears to attach devices as if there were a direct connection.
- Dedicated communication path between two stations. Path is a connected sequence of links between network nodes.
- On each physical link, a logical channel is dedicated to the connection. Communication via circuit switching involves three phases:

    ○ Circuit Establishment
    ○ Data Transfer
    ○ Circuit Disconnect

- Connection path must be established before data transmission begins. Nodes must have switching capacity and channel capacity to establish connection.
- Switches must have intelligence to work out routing.

Packet Switching

- Packet switching was designed to provide a more efficient facility than circuit-switching for bursty data traffic.
- With packet switching, a station transmits data in small blocks, called packets.
- At each node packets are received, stored briefly (buffered) and passed on to the next node.

    ○ Store and forward mechanism

- Each packet contains some portion of the user data plus control info needed for proper functioning of the network.
- A key element of packet-switching networks is whether the internal operation is datagram or virtual circuit (VC).

    ○ With internal VCs, a route is defined between two endpoints and all packets for that VC follow the same route.

- ○ With internal diagrams, each packet is treated independently, and packets intended for the same destination may follow different routes.

Examples of packet switching networks are X.25, Frame Relay, ATM and IP.

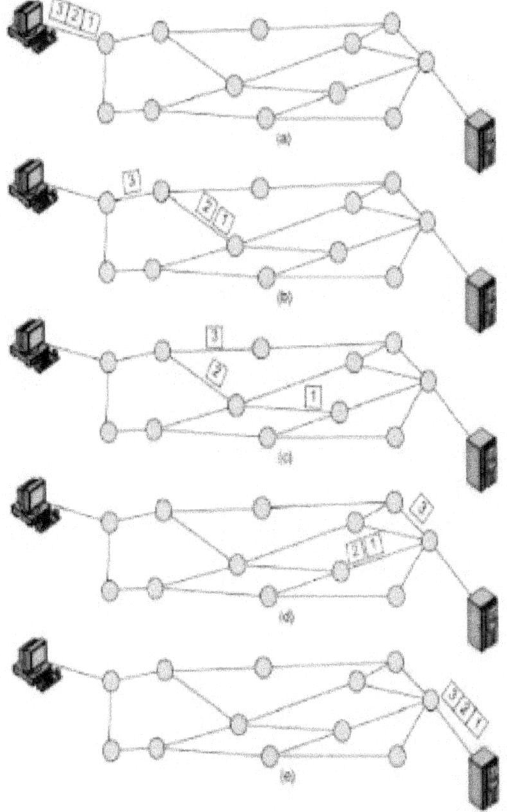

Figure 21: Packet Switching

- Station breaks long message into packets. Packets sent one at a time to the network.
- Packets handled in two ways:

1. Datagram

    - Each packet treated independently
    - Packets can take any practical route
    - Packets may arrive out of order
    - Packets may go missing
    - Up to receiver to re-order packets and recover from missing packets

2. Virtual Circuit

    - Preplanned route established before any packets sent.
    - Once route is established, all the packets between the two communicating parties follow the same route through the network
    - Call request and call accept packets establish connection (handshake)
    - Each packet contains a Virtual Circuit Identifier (VCI) instead of destination address
    - No routing decisions required for each packet
    - Clear request to drop circuit
    - Not a dedicated path

What is Protocol?

- A protocol defines rules and conventions for communication between network devices.
- A protocol defines the format and the order of messages exchanged between two or more communicating entities, as well as the actions taken on the transmission and/or receipt of a message or other event.

- The key features of protocol are as follows:
- **Syntax**: Concerns the format of the data blocks
- **Semantics**: Includes control information for coordination and error handling
- **Timing**: Includes speed matching and sequencing
- **Example**: HTTP, IP, FTP etc...

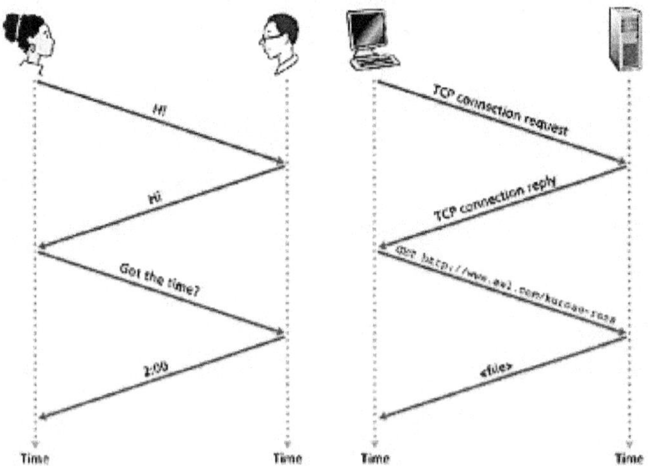

Figure 22: A human protocol and a computer network protocol

- It defines those computers of the network used at the edge of the network. These computers are known as hosts or end system.
- Host can be classified into the following two types:

  - **Clients**: Refer to the computer systems that request servers for the completion of a task. The clients are generally called desktop PCs or workstations.
  - **Servers**: Refer to the computer systems that receive requests from the clients and process them. After the processing is

complete, the servers send a reply to the clients who sent the request.

- The concept of clients and servers is essential in the network design. The various networks design models are as follows:

Peer to Peer network

- A group of computers is connected together so that users can share resources and information.
- There is no central location for authenticating users, storing files, or accessing resources.
- This means that users must remember which computers in the workgroup have the shared resource or information that they want to access.
- Advantage:

  ○ It is easy to setup.
  ○ There is no need of any committed server as each peer acts as both server and client.
  ○ The network implementation is quite cheap.
  ○ The resources of a peer can be shared with other peers very easily in the network.

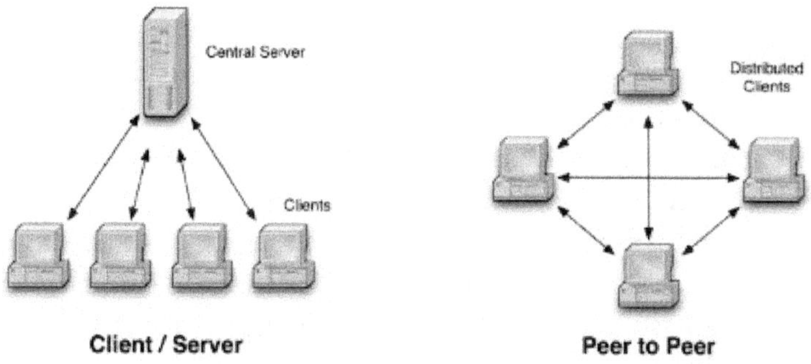

Figure 23: Network Edge - Peer to Peer and Client/Server Network

- Disadvantage:

  - The speed of the network decreases due to heavy usage.
  - It is not easy to keep track of information on each computer.
  - There is on central backup of files and folders.
  - Network and data security are weak.

Client/Server network

- A client/server network is a system where one or more computers called clients connect to a central computer named a server to share or use resources.
- The client requests a service from server, which may include running an application, querying database, printing a document, or performing a backup or recovery procedure. The request made by the client is held by server.
- A client/server network is that the files and resources are centralized. This means that a computer, the server, can hold them and other computers can access them.
- Advantage:

- ◦ The server system holds the shared files.
- ◦ The server system can be scheduled to take the file backups automatically.
- ◦ Network access is provided only to authorize users through user security at the server.
- ◦ The server system is a kind of central repository for sharing printer with clients.
- ◦ Internet access, e-mail routing, and such other networking tasks are quite easily managed by the server.
- ◦ The software applications shared by the server are accessible to the clients.

- • Disadvantage:

  - ◦ The implementation of the network is quite expensive.
  - ◦ A network operating system is essential.
  - ◦ If server fails, the entire network crashes.

Protocols layers and their service model

OSI Layer Architecture

- • OSI model is based on a proposal developed by the International Standards Organization (ISO) as a first step toward international standardization of the protocols used in the various layers.
- • It was revised in 1995.
- • The model is called the ISO OSI (Open Systems Interconnection) Reference Model because it deals with connecting open systems—that is, systems that are open for communication with other systems.
- • The OSI model has seven layers.

  1. Physical Layer 2. Data Link Layer
  3. Network Layer 4. Transport Layer

5. Session Layer 6. Presentation Layer
7. Application Layer
Physical Layer

- The physical layer coordinates the function required to carry a bit stream over a physical medium.
- It deals with the mechanical and electrical specifications of the interface and transmission medium.
- It also defines the procedures and functions that physical devices and interfaces have to perform for transmission to occur.
- The physical layer is concerned with the following:

  - Physical characteristics of interface and medium
  - Representation of bits
  - Data rate
  - Synchronization of bits
  - Line configuration
  - Physical topology
  - Transmission mode

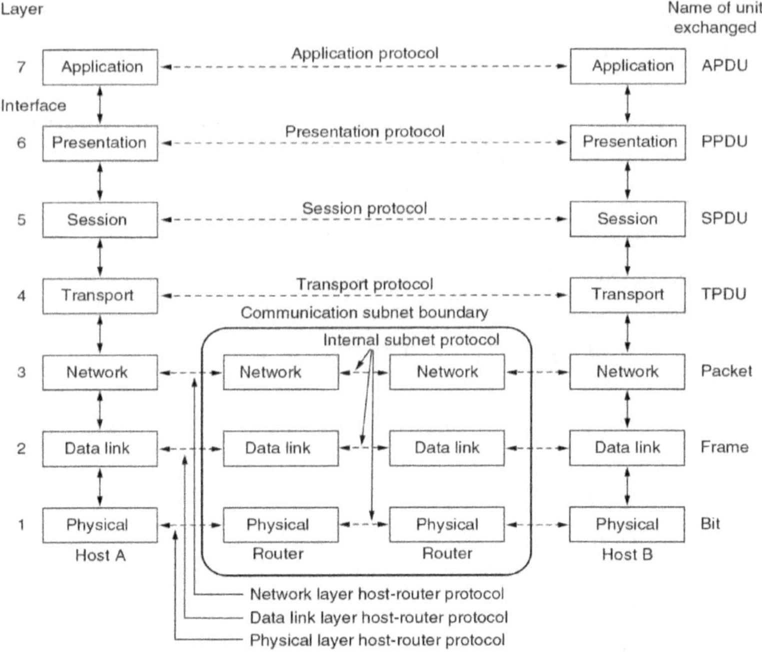

Figure 24: OSI Reference Model

Data Link Layer

- The data link layer transforms the physical layer, a raw transmission facility, to a reliable link.
- It makes the physical layer appear error-free to the upper layer.
- The data link layer is concerned with the following:

  ○ Framing
  ○ Physical addressing
  ○ Flow control
  ○ Error control
  ○ Access control

Network Layer

- The network layer is responsible for the source-to-destination delivery of a packet, possibly across multiple networks.
- The network layer is concerned with the following:

  - Logical addressing
  - Routing

Transport Layer

- The transport layer is responsible for process-to-process delivery of the entire message.
- A process is an application program running on a host.
- The transport layer ensures that the whole message arrives intact and in order, overseeing both error control and flow control at the source-to-destination level.
- The transport layer is concerned with the following:

  - Service-point addressing
  - Segmentation and reassembly
  - Connection control
  - Flow control
  - Error control

Session Layer

- The session layer is the network dialog controller.
- It establishes, maintains, and synchronizes the interaction among communicating systems.
- The session layer is concerned with the following:

  - Dialog control
  - Synchronization

Presentation Layer

- The presentation layer is concerned with the syntax (language rule) and semantics (meaning of each rule) of the information exchanged between two systems.
- The presentation layer is concerned with the following:

  - Translation
  - Encryption
  - Compression

Application Layer

- The application layer enables the user, whether human or software, to access the network.
- It provides user interfaces and support for services such as electronic mail, remote file access and transfer, shared database management, and other types of distributed information services.
- The application layer is concerned with the following:
- Network virtual terminal

  - File transfer, access, and management
  - Mail services
  - Directory services

TCP/IP Reference Model

- Transmission Control Protocol/Internet Protocol (TCP/IP) protocol suite is the engine for the Internet and networks worldwide.
- TCP/IP either combines several OSI layers into a single layer, or does not use certain layers at all.

- TCP/IP is a set of protocols developed to allow cooperating computers to share resources across the network.
- The TCP/IP model has five layers.

1. Application Layer
2. Transport Layer
3. Internet Layer
4. Data Link Layer
5. Physical Network

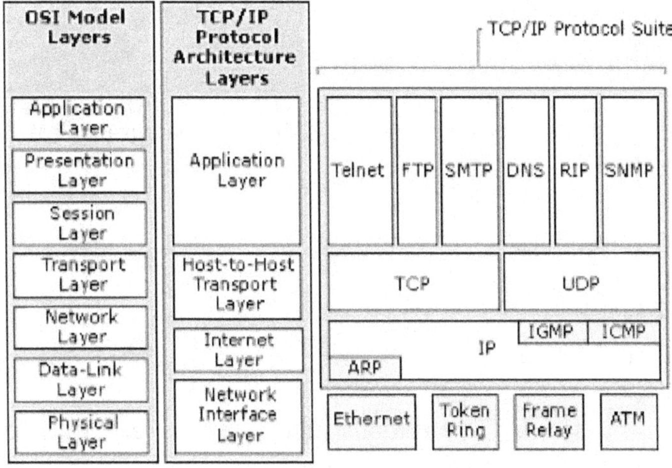

Figure 25: TCP/IP Reference Model

Application Layer

- The application layer is provided by the program that uses TCP/IP for communication.
- An application is a user process cooperating with another process usually on a different host (there is also a benefit to application communication within a single host).

- **Examples**: Telnet and the File Transfer Protocol (FTP) etc...

Transport Layer

- The transport layer provides the end-to-end data transfer by delivering data from an application to its remote peer.
- Multiple applications can be supported simultaneously.
- The most-used transport layer protocol is the Transmission Control Protocol (TCP), which provides:

  - Connection-oriented reliable data delivery
  - Duplicate data suppression
  - Congestion control
  - Flow control.

- Another transport layer protocol is the User Datagram Protocol (UDP), which provides:

  - Connectionless
  - Unreliable

  - Best-effort service.

- UDP is used by applications that need a fast transport mechanism and can tolerate the loss of some data.

Internetwork Layer

- The internetwork layer also called the internet layer or the network layer.
- It is provides the "virtual network" image of an internet this layer shields the higher levels from the physical network architecture below it.
- Internet Protocol (IP) is the most important protocol in this layer.

- It is a connectionless protocol that does not assume reliability from lower layers. IP does not provide reliability, flow control, or error recovery.
- IP provides a routing function that attempts to deliver transmitted messages to their destination.
- These message units in an IP network are called an IP datagram.
- **Example**: IP, ICMP, IGMP, ARP, and RARP.

Network Interface Layer

- The network interface layer, also called the link layer or the data-link layer or Host to Network Layer.
- It is the interface to the actual network hardware. This interface may or may not provide reliable delivery, and may be packet or stream oriented.
- **Example**: IEEE 802.2, X.25,ATM, FDDI

Physical Network Layer

- The physical network layer specifies the characteristics of the hardware to be used for the network.
- **For example**, it specifies:

  - The physical characteristics of the communications media
  - Standards such as IEEE 802.3
  - The specification for Ethernet network media, and RS-232
  - The specification for standard pin connectors.

Internetworking

- An interconnected set of networks may appear simply as a larger network. This entire configuration is often referred to as an internet.

Internetworking Terms

- **Communication Network:**

  - A facility that provides a data transfer service among devices attached to the network.

- Internet:

  - A collection of communication networks interconnected by bridge and /or routers.

- Intranet:

  - An internet used by single organization that provides the key Internet application, especially the World Wide Web.
  - An intranet operates within the organization for internal purpose and can exist as an isolated, self-contained internet, or may have links to the internet.

- End Systems:

  - A device attached to one of the networks of an internet that is used to support end-user application or services.

- Intermediate System:

  - A device used to connect two networks and permit communication between end systems attached to different networks.

- Bridge:

  - A bridge is a type of computer network device that provides interconnection with other bridge networks that use the same protocol.

- Bridge devices work at the data link layer of the Open System Interconnect (OSI) model, connecting two different networks together and providing communication between them.
- Bridges are similar to repeaters and hubs in that they broadcast data to every node.
- However, bridges maintain the media access control (MAC) address table as soon as they discover new segments, so subsequent transmissions are sent to only to the desired recipient.
- Bridges are also known as Layer 2 switches.

- Router:

  - A router is a device that analyzes the contents of data packets transmitted within a network or to another network.
  - Routers determine whether the source and destination are on the same network or whether data must be transferred from one network type to another, which requires encapsulating the data packet with routing protocol header information.
  - Router operates at layer 3 of the OSI model.

2
Cellular Wireless Network

Antennas and Propagation

Introduction:

- Two persons, who need to convey a thought, an idea or a doubt, can do so by voice communication.
- Here, communication takes place through **sound waves**. However, if two people want to communicate who is at longer distances, then we have to convert these sound waves into **electromagnetic waves**.
- The device, which converts the required information signal into electromagnetic waves, is known as an **Antenna**.
- **An Antenna** is a transducer, which converts electrical power into electromagnetic waves and vice versa.
- An Antenna can be used either as a transmitting antenna or a receiving antenna.
- A transmitting an antenna is one, which converts electrical signals into electromagnetic waves and radiates them.
- A receiving an antenna is one, which converts electromagnetic waves from the received beam into electrical signals.
- In two-way communication, the same antenna can be used for both transmission and reception.

- Radiation Patterns
- An antenna will radiate power in all directions but, does not perform equally well in all directions.
- A common way to characterize the performance of an antenna is the radiation pattern, which is a graphical representation of the radiation properties of an antenna as a function of space coordinates.
- The simplest pattern is produced by an idealized antenna known as the **isotropic antenna**.
- An isotropic antenna is a point in space that radiates power in all directions equally.
- The actual radiation pattern for the isotropic antenna is a sphere with the antenna at the center.
- However, radiation patterns are almost always depicted as a two-dimensional cross section of the three-dimensional pattern.
-

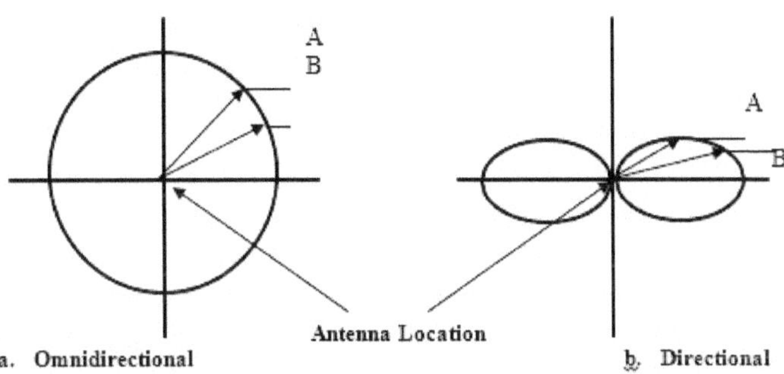

Figure 1: Idealized Radiation Patterns

- The pattern for the isotropic antenna is shown in Figure 1a.
- The distance from the antenna to each point on the radiation pattern is proportional to the power radiated from the antenna

in that direction.

- Figure 1b shows the radiation pattern of another idealized antenna. This is a directional antenna in which the preferred direction of radiation is along one axis.

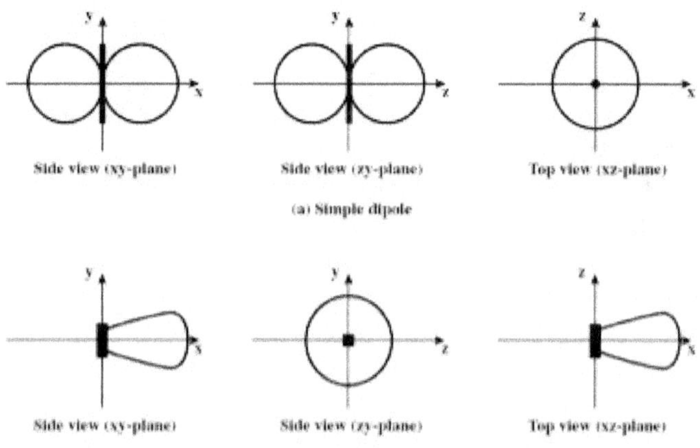

Figure 2: Radiation Patterns in Three Dimensions

- The relative distance determines the relative power.
- To determine the relative power in a given direction, a line is drawn from the antenna position at the appropriate angle, and the point of intercept with the radiation pattern is determined.
- Figure 1 shows a comparison of two transmission angles, A and B, drawn on the two radiation patterns.
- The isotropic antenna produces an omnidirectional radiation pattern of equal strength in all directions, so the A and B vectors are of equal length.
- For the antenna pattern of Figure 1b, the B vector is longer than the A vector, indicating that more power is radiated in the B

direction than in the A direction, and the relative lengths of the two vectors are proportional to the amount of power radiated in the two directions.

Types of Antennas

- **Dipoles**
- Two of the simplest and most basic antennas are the half-wave dipole antenna (Figure 3) and the quarter-wave vertical, or Marconi, antenna (Figure 3).
- The half-wave dipole consists of two straight collinear conductors of equal length, separated by a small gap.
- The length of the antenna is one-half the wavelength of the signal that can be transmitted most efficiently.
- A vertical quarter wave antenna is the type commonly used for automobile radios and portable radios.
- A half-wave dipole has a uniform or omnidirectional radiation pattern in one dimension and a figure eight pattern in the other two dimensions (Figure -2).

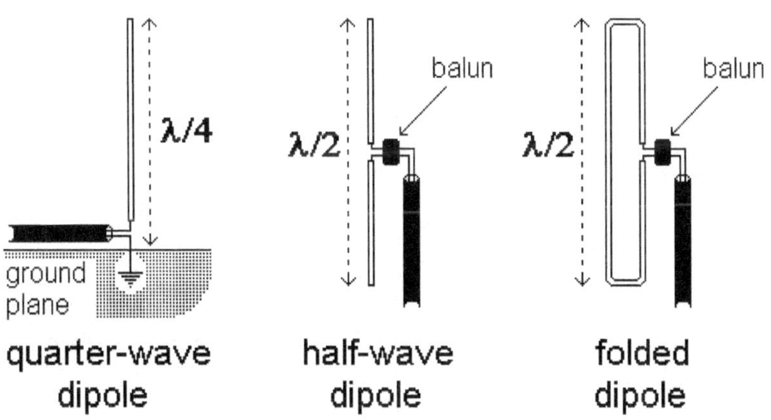

Figure 3: Type of Antenna

1. Parabolic Reflective Antenna

- An important type of antenna is the parabolic reflective antenna, which is used in terrestrial microwave and satellite applications.
- A parabola is the locus of all points equidistant from a fixed line and a fixed point not on the line.
- The fixed point is called the focus and the fixed line is called the directrix (Figure 4a).

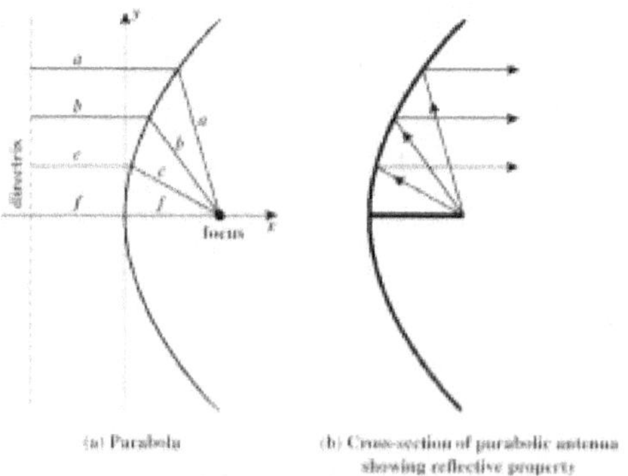

Figure 4: Parabolic Antenna

- If a parabola is revolved about its axis, the surface generated is called a paraboloid.
- A cross section through the paraboloid parallel to its axis forms a parabola and a cross section perpendicular to the axis forms a circle.
- Such surfaces are used in automobile headlights, optical and radio telescopes, and microwave antennas. Figure 4b shows this effect in cross section.

Antenna Gain

- Antenna gain is a measure of the directionality of an antenna.
- Antenna gain is defined as the power output, in a particular direction, compared to that produced in any direction by a perfect omnidirectional antenna (isotropic antenna).
- A concept related to that of antenna gain is the effective area of an antenna.
- The effective area of an antenna is related to the physical size of the antenna and to its shape.
- The relationship between antenna gain and effective area is:

$$G = 4\,\frac{\pi A e}{\lambda 2} = 4\,\frac{\pi f 2 A e}{c 2}$$

Where:

G = antenna gain
Ae = effective area
f = carrier frequency
c = speed of light (3*108 m/s)
$\square$ = carrier wavelength

Propagation Modes in Wireless Communication

- In the earth environment, electromagnetic waves propagate in ways that depend own properties but also on those of the environment itself.
- The various methods of propagation depend largely on frequency.
- A signal radiated from an antenna travels along one of three routes:

1. Ground Wave
2. Sky Wave

1. Line of Sight (LOS)

1. Ground Wave

- Radio waves in the VLF band propagate in a ground, or surface wave. The wave is connected at one end to the surface of the earth and to the ionosphere at the other.
- The ionosphere is the region above the troposphere (where the air is), from about 50 to 250 miles above the earth.
- It is a collection of ions, which are atoms that have some of their electrons stripped off leaving two or more electrically charged objects. The sun's rays cause the ions to form which slowly modified.

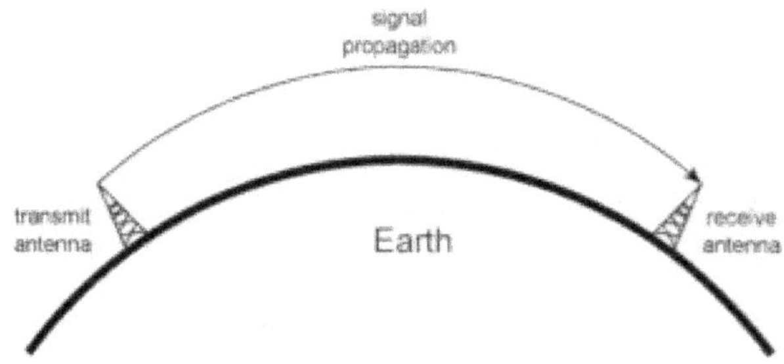

Figure 5: Ground Wave Propagation

- The propagation of radio waves in the presence of ions is drastically different than in air, which is why the ionosphere plays an important role in most modes of propagation.
- Ground waves travel between two limits, the earth and the ionosphere, which acts like a channel. Since the channel curves with the earth, the ground wave will follow. Therefore very long range propagation is possible using ground waves.
- Example of ground wave communication is AM radio.

1. Sky Waves

- Radio waves in the LF and MF ranges may also propagate as ground waves, but suffer significant losses, or are attenuated, particularly at higher frequencies. But as the ground wave mode fades out, a new mode develops: the sky wave.
- Sky waves are reflections from the ionosphere. While the wave is in the ionosphere, it is strongly bent, or refracted, ultimately back to the ground.
- From a long distance away this appears as a reflection. Long ranges are possible in this mode also, up to hundreds of miles.

- Sky waves in this frequency band are usually only possible at night, when the concentration of ions is not too great since the ionosphere also tends to attenuate the signal.

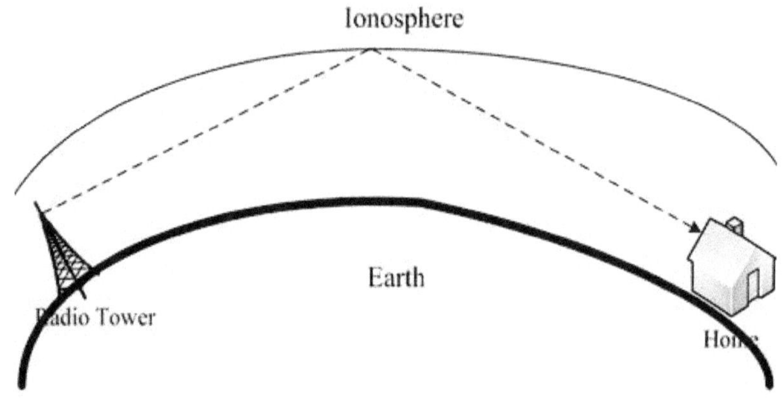

Figure 6: Sky Wave Propagation

- However, at night, there are just enough ions to reflect the wave but not reduce its power too much.
- Example: Used in amateur radio, CB radio, international broadcast such as BBC.

1. Line-of-sight propagation

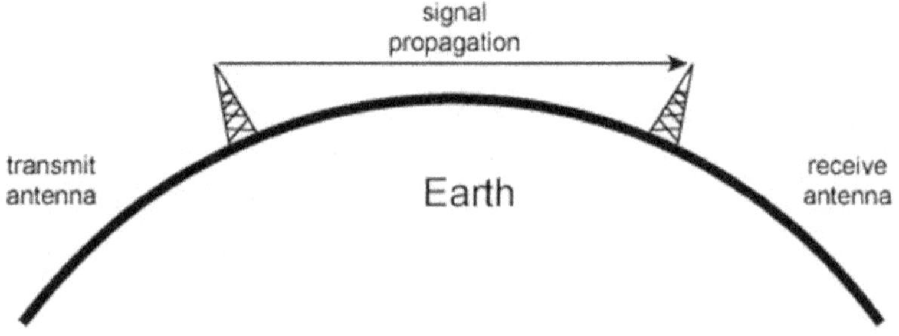

Figure 7:Line-of-sight propagation

- Transmitting and receiving antennas must be within line of sight.

    1. Satellite communication – signal above 30 MHz not reflected by ionosphere
    2. Ground communication – antennas within effective line of site due to refraction

- Refraction – bending of microwaves by the atmosphere.

1. Velocity of electromagnetic wave is a function of the density of the medium
2. When wave changes medium, speed changes
3. Wave bends at the boundary between mediums Optical and Radio line of sight

$? = ?. ??\sqrt{?}$ **and** $? = ?. ??\sqrt{??}$

Where:

d = distance between antenna and horizon (km) h = antenna height (m)

K = adjustment factor to account for refraction, rule of thumb K = 4/3

- Maximum distance between two antennas for LOS propagation:

$= ?. ?(4??_? + 4??_?)$

Where:

h1 = height of antenna one h2 = height of antenna two

Line-Of-Sight Transmission

- Line of sight (LoS) is a type of propagation that can transmit and receive data only where transmit and receive stations are in view of each other without any sort of an obstacle between them.

- FM radio, microwave and satellite transmission are examples of line-of-sight communication.
- We have examined various impairments on the information-carrying capacity of a communications link.
- The most significant impairments are:

1. Attenuation and Attenuation distortion

- Strength of signal falls off with distance over transmission medium.
- Attenuation introduces three factors for unguided media:

   1. Received signal must have sufficient strength so that circuitry in the receiver can interpret the signal.
   2. Signal must maintain a level sufficiently higher than noise to be received without error.
   3. Attenuation is greater at higher frequencies, causing distortion.

1. Free space loss

- For any type of wireless communication the signal disperses with distance. Therefore, an antenna with a fixed area will receive less signal power the farther it is from the transmitting antenna.
- For satellite communication this is the primary mode of signal loss. Even if no other sources of attenuation or impairment are assumed, a transmitted signal attenuates over distance because the signal is being spread over a larger and larger area.
- This form of attenuation is known as **free space loss**, which can be express in terms of the ratio of the radiated power "Pt to the power p, received by the antenna or, in decibels, by taking 10 times the log of that ratio.
- For the ideal isotropic antenna, free space loss is:

$$\frac{P_t}{P_r} = \frac{(4\pi d)^2}{\lambda^2} = \frac{(4\pi f d)^2}{c^2}$$

Where:
Pt = signal power at transmitting antenna
Pr = signal power at receiving antenna
$\square$ = carrier wavelength
d = propagation distance between antennasc
= speed of light (3 * 10^8 m/s)

Where d and $\square$ are in the same units (e.g., meters)
- Free space loss equation can be recast:

$$L_{dB} = 10\log\frac{P_t}{P_r} = 20\log\left(\frac{4\pi d}{\lambda}\right)$$
$$= -20\log(\lambda) + 20\log(d) + 21.98\ dB$$
$$= 20\log\left\lfloor\frac{4\pi f d}{c}\right\rfloor$$
$$= 20\log(f) + 20\log(d) - 147.56 dB$$

- Free space loss accounting for gain of other antennas

$$\frac{P_t}{P_r} = \frac{(4\pi)^2(d)^2}{G_r G_t \lambda^2} = \frac{(\lambda d)^2}{A_r A_t} = \frac{(cd)^2}{f^2 A_r A_t}$$

Where
Gt = gain of transmitting antenna
Gr = gain of receiving antenna
At = effective area of transmitting antenna
Ar = effective area of receiving antenna

- Free space loss accounting for gain of other antennas can be recast as:

$$L_{dB} = 20\log(\lambda) + 20\log(d) - 10\log(A_t A_r)$$
$$= -20\log(f) + 20\log(d) - 10\log(A_t A_r) + 169.54 dB$$

1. Noise

A. **Thermal Noise:**

- Thermal noise due to agitation of electrons.
- It is present in all electronic devices and transmission media and is a function of temperature.
- Thermal noise is uniformly distributed across the frequency spectrum and hence is often referred to as white noise.
- It cannot be eliminated and therefore places an upper bound on communications system performance.
- It is particularly significant for satellite communication.
- Amount of thermal noise to be found in a bandwidth of 1Hz in any device or conductor is:

$$N_0 = kT\left(\frac{W}{H_z}\right)$$

Where:
N_0 = noise power density in watts per 1 Hz of bandwidth
k = Boltzmann's constant = 1.38 x 10-23 J/K
T = temperature, in kelvins (absolute temperature)
Noise is assumed to be independent of frequency.
Thermal noise present in a bandwidth of B Hertz (in watts):

$$N = kTB$$

Or, in decibel-watts
? = ?? ??? ? + ?? ??? ? + ?? ??? ?

$$= -???.\ ???? + ??\ ???\ ? + ??\ ???\ ?$$

A. **Intermodulation noise**

- It occurs if signals with different frequencies share the same medium.
- Interference caused by a signal produced at a frequency that is the sum or difference of original frequencies.
- Intermodulation noise is produced when there is some nonlinearity in the transmitter receiver, or intervening transmission system.
- Normally, these components behave as linear systems; that is, the output is equal to the input times a constant.

A. **Crosstalk**

- Crosstalk has been experienced by anyone who, while using the telephone, has been able to hear another conversation; it is an unwanted coupling between signal paths.
- It can occur by electrical coupling between nearby twisted pairs or, rarely, coax cable lines carrying multiple signals.
- Crosstalk can also occur when unwanted signals are picked up by microwave antennas; although highly directional antennas are used, microwave energy does spread during propagation.
- Typically, crosstalk is of the same order of magnitude as, or less than, thermal noise. However, in the unlicensed ISM bands, crosstalk often dominates.
- Impulse noise
- It is non-continuous, consisting of irregular pulses or noise spikes of short duration and of relatively high amplitude.
- It is generated from a variety of causes, including external electromagnetic disturbances, such as lightning, and faults and flaws in the communications system.
- Impulse noise is generally only a minor annoyance for analog data.

- For example, voice transmission may be corrupted by short clicks and crackles with no loss of intelligibility.
- However, impulse noise is the primary source of error in digital data transmission.
- For example, a sharp spike of energy of 0.01 s duration would not destroy any voice data but would wash out about 560 bits of data being transmitted at 56 kbps.

Multipath Propagation & Fading in the Mobile Environment

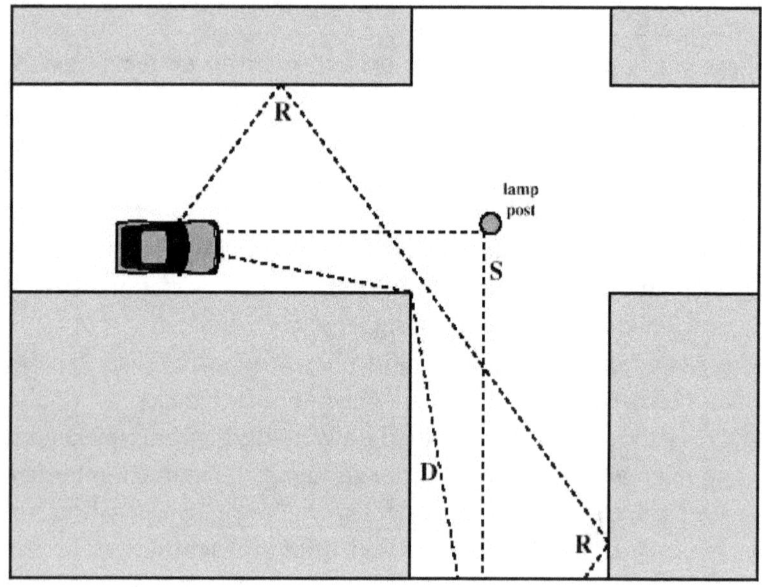

Figure 8: Propagation Mechanism (Reflection, Diffraction, Scattering)

- **Reflection** - occurs when signal encounters a surface that is large relative to the wavelength of the signal.
- **Diffraction** - occurs at the edge of an impenetrable body that is large compared to wavelength of radio wave.

- **Scattering**– occurs when incoming signal hits an object whose size in the order of the wavelength of the signal or less.

The Effects of Multipath Propagation

- Multiple copies of a signal may arrive at different phases.
- If phases add destructively, the signal level relative to noise declines, making detection more difficult.
- Inter symbol interference (ISI); one or more delayed copies of a pulse may arrive at the same time as the primary pulse for a subsequent bit.

Fading

- The term fading, or, small-scale fading, means rapid fluctuations of the amplitudes, phases, or multipath delays of a radio signal over a short period or short travel distance.
- This might be so severe that large scale radio propagation loss effects might be ignored.

Multipath Fading Effects:

- Rapid changes in signal strength over a small travel distance or time interval.
- Random frequency modulation due to varying Doppler shifts on different multipath signals.
- Time dispersion or echoes caused by multipath propagation delays.

Factors Influencing Fading:

- Few physical factors influence small-scale fading in the radio propagation channel like;

A. Multipath Propagation:

- Multipath is the propagation phenomenon that results in radio signals reaching the receiving antenna by two or more paths. The effects of multipath include constructive and destructive interference, and phase shifting of the signal.

A. Speed of the mobile:

- The relative motion between the base station and the mobile results in random frequency modulation due to different Doppler shifts on each of the multipath components.

C. Speed of surrounding objects:

- If objects in the radio channel are in motion, they induce a time varying Doppler shift on multipath components. If the surrounding objects move at a greater rate than the mobile, then this effect dominates fading.

D. Transmission Bandwidth of the signal

- If the transmitted radio signal bandwidth is greater than the "bandwidth" of the multipath channel (quantified by coherence bandwidth), the received signal will be distorted.

Types of Small-Scale Fading:

- The type of fading experienced by the signal through a mobile channel depends on the relation between the signal parameters (bandwidth, symbol period) and the channel parameters (rms delay spread and Doppler spread).
- Hence we have four different types of fading. There are two types of fading due to the time dispersive nature of the channel.

Fading Effects due to Multipath Time Delay Spread:

1. **Flat Fading:**

- Such types of fading occur when the bandwidth of the transmitted signal is less than the coherence bandwidth of the channel. Equivalently if the symbol period of the signal is more than the rms delay spread of the channel, then the fading is at fading.
- So we can say that at fading occurs when;

BS << BC

Where BS is the signal bandwidth and BC is the coherence bandwidth. Also,

TS >>$\sigma\tau$

Where TS is the symbol period and $\sigma\tau$ is the rms delay spread. And in such a case, mobile channel has a constant gain and linear phase response over its bandwidth.

2. Frequency Selective Fading:

- Frequency selective fading occurs when the signal bandwidth is more than the coherence bandwidth of the mobile radio channel or equivalently the symbols duration of the signal is less than the rms delay spread.

BS >> BC and TS <<$\sigma\tau$

- At the receiver, we obtain multiple copies of the transmitted signal, all attenuated and delayed in time. The channel introduces inter symbol interference.
- A rule of thumb for a channel to have at fading is if $\sigma\tau$ /TS<= 0.1

Fading Effects due to Doppler Spread:

1. **Fast Fading:**

- In a fast fading channel, the channel impulse response changes rapidly within the symbol duration of the signal. Due to Doppler spreading, signal undergoes frequency dispersion leading to distortion. Therefore a signal undergoes fast fading if

TS >> TC
Where TC is the coherence time and
BS >> BD
Where BD is the Doppler spread. Transmission involving very low data rates suffers from fast fading.

2. Slow Fading:

- In such a channel, the rate of the change of the channel impulse response is much less than the transmitted signal.
- We can consider a slow faded channel a channel in which channel is almost constant over at least one symbol duration. Hence

TS << TC and BS >> BD

- We observe that the velocity of the user plays an important role in deciding whether the signal experiences fast or slow fading.

Encoding and Modulation

Basics:

- For digital signaling, Data source g(t) which may be either digital or analog, is encoded into digital signal x(t).
- Actually, its depends on encoding technique.
- For analog signaling, continuous constant-frequency signal known as a carrier signal.
- Data can transmit using a carrier signal by modulation.

- **Modulation** is the process of encoding source data onto a carrier signal with frequency fc.
- The frequency of the carrier signal is chosen to be compatible with the transmission medium being used.

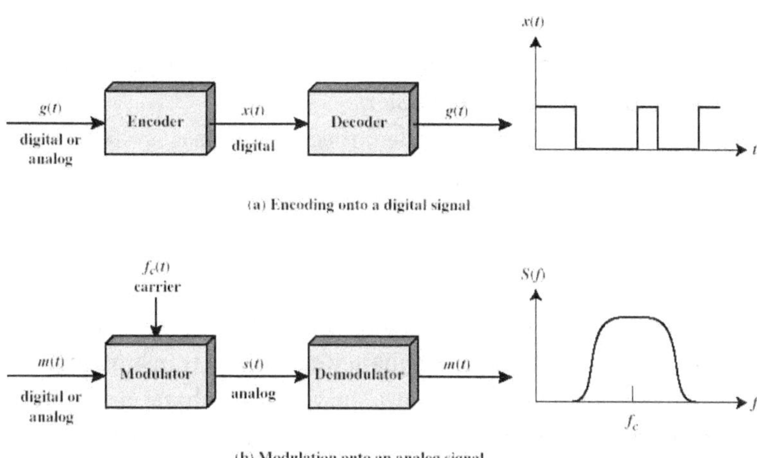

Figure 9: Modulation (Analog and Digital)

- According to the input source signal m(t) (either analog or digital), which is called baseband signal (or modulating signal) , the carrier signal fc(t) will be modulated into modulated signal s(t).
- Modulation techniques involve operation on one or more of the three parameters:

  A. Amplitude
  B. Frequency
  C. Phase

- Total four different mappings or encodings techniques available:

1. digital-to-digital
2. digital-to-analog
3. analog-to-analog
4. analog-to-digital

Digital-to-analog

- Digital data and digital signals must be converted to analog signals for wireless transmission.
- Optical system and unguided media (wireless system) only propagate analog signals.

Analog-to-analog

- A baseband analog signal, such as voice or video, must be modulated onto a higher-frequency carrier for transmission.
- Baseband: easy and cheap, e.g., in voice telephone lines, voice signals are transmitted over telephone lines at their original spectrum.

Analog-to-digital

- Conversion of analog data (e.g., voice, video) to digital form permits the use of modern digital transmission & switching.
- It's a common to digitize voice signals prior to transmission over either guided or unguided media to improve quality and to take advantage of TDM scheme.

Signal Encoding Criteria

- Signal encoding schemes can be compared on certain criteria such as:

1. **Signal Spectrum** – Bandwidth requirements for a given data rate.

2. **Clocking** – The receiver must determine the beginning and end of each bit. Need to synchronizing transmitter and receiver. Use external clock, which is expensive. Synchronization mechanism based on the transmitted signal.

3. **Signal interference and noise immunity** - Some codes are better than others in the presence of noise. Performance is usually expressed in terms of BER.

Digital data, Analog signal

- To transmitting digital data using analog signal.
- Most familiar use of this transformation is Public telephone system.

- Designed to transmit analog signals in 300Hz to 3400Hz.
- Use modem for digital data to analog, vice versa. (modulator-demodulator)

- Modulation involves operation on one or more of the three characteristics of a carrier signal.

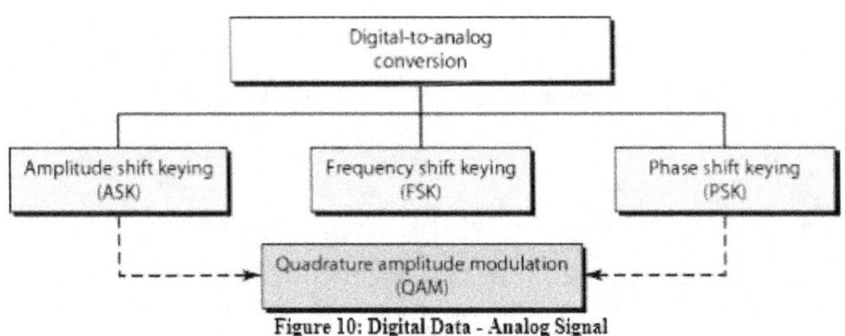

Figure 10: Digital Data - Analog Signal

1. Amplitude Shift Keying

- Amplitude Shift Keying (ASK) is a type of Amplitude Modulation which represents the binary data in the form of variations in the amplitude of a signal.
- Any modulated signal has a high frequency carrier.
- The binary signal when ASK modulated, gives a zero value for Low input while it gives the carrier output for High input.
- The following figure represents ASK modulated waveform along with its input.

- Both frequency & phase remain constant while amplitude changes and one of the amplitudes is zero.
- Inefficient because Up to 1200bps on voice grade lines.
- **Application**: ASK is used to transmit digital data over optical fiber.

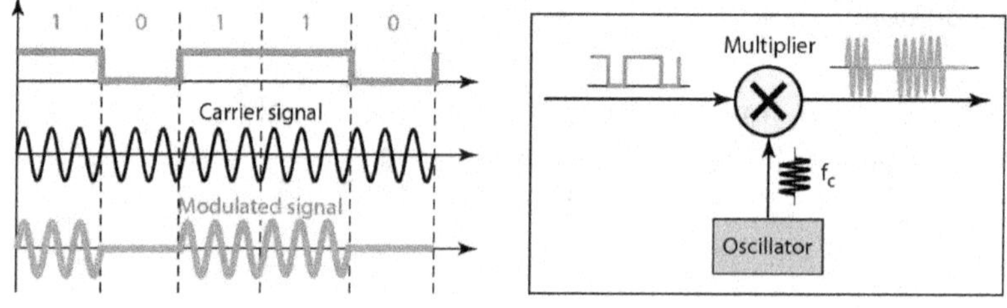

Figure 11: Amplitude Shift Keying

- The ASK modulator block diagram comprises of the carrier signal generator, the binary sequence from the message signal and the band-limited filter. Above is the diagram of the ASK Modulator.

1. Frequency Shift Keying

- Frequency Shift Keying (FSK) is the digital modulation technique in which the frequency of the carrier signal varies according to the digital signal changes.
- The most common form of FSK is binary FSK (BFSK).
- FSK is a scheme of frequency modulation.
- The output of a FSK modulated wave is high in frequency for a binary High input and is low in frequency for a binary Low input. The binary 1s and 0s are called Mark and Space frequencies.
- The following image is the diagrammatic representation of FSK modulated waveform along with its input.

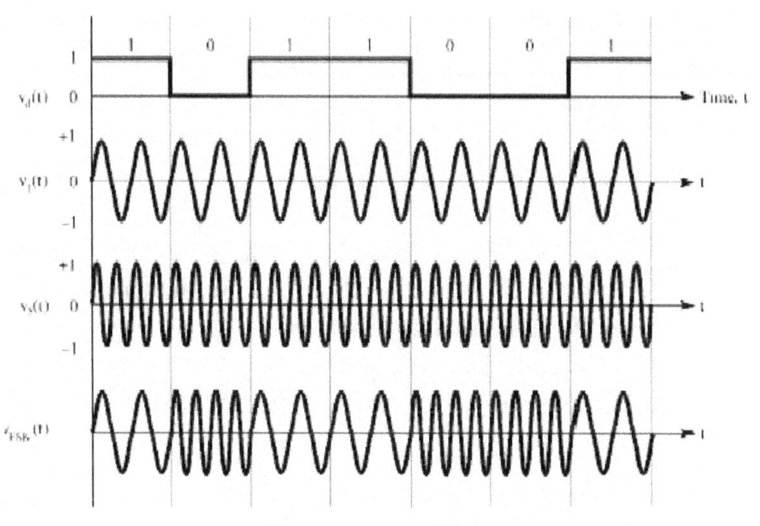

Figure 12: Frequency Shift Keying

- Peak amplitude & phase remain constant during each bit interval.
- BFSK is less susceptible to error than ASK.

- **Application**: it is used over voice lines, high frequency (3 to 30MHz) radio transmission.

1. Phase Shift Keying

- Phase Shift Keying (PSK) is the digital modulation technique in which the phase of the carrier signal is changed by varying the sine and cosine inputs at a particular time.
- PSK technique is widely used for wireless LANs, bio-metric, contactless operations, along with RFID and Bluetooth communications.
- Peak amplitude & freq. remain constant during each bit interval.
- More efficient use of bandwidth (higher data-rate) are possible, compared to FSK.
- PSK is of two types, depending upon the phases the signal gets shifted. They are –

    1. Binary Phase Shift Keying (BPSK)

        - This is also called as 2-phase PSK or Phase Reversal Keying. In this technique, the sine wave carrier takes two phase reversals such as 0° and 180°.
        - BPSK is basically a Double Side Band Suppressed Carrier (DSBSC) modulation scheme, for message being the digital information.

    2. Quadrature Phase Shift Keying (QPSK)

        - This is the phase shift keying technique, in which the sine wave carrier takes four phase reversals such as 0°, 90°, 180°, and 270°.
        - If this kind of techniques are further extended, PSK can be done by eight or sixteen values also, depending upon the requirement.

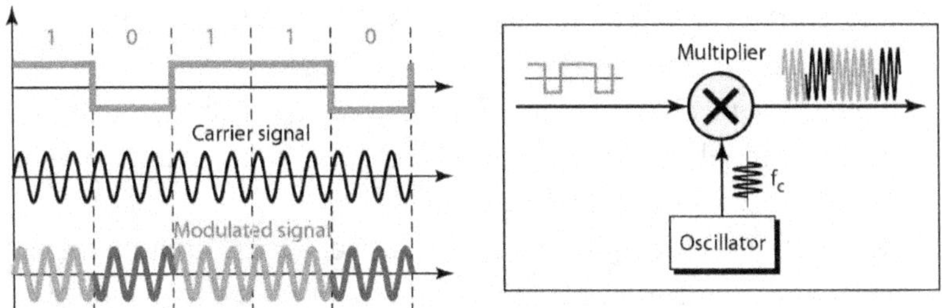

Figure 13: Phase Shift Keying

- The diagram of Binary Phase Shift Keying consists of the balance modulator which has the carrier sine wave as one input and the binary sequence as the other input.

Analog Data, Analog Signals

- Modulation is combine an input signal m(t) and a carrier frequency fc to produce a signal s(t) whose bandwidth is usually centered on fc.
- E.g., voice signals are transmitted over telephone lines at their original spectrum.
- Types of modulation

1. Angle Modulation

   A. Frequency modulation - FM
   B. Phase modulation - PM

2. Amplitude Modulation – AM

- A continuous-wave goes on continuously without any intervals and it is the baseband message signal, which contains the information. This wave has to be modulated.
- According to the standard definition, "The amplitude of the carrier signal varies in accordance with the instantaneous amplitude of the modulating signal."
- Means that the amplitude of the carrier signal containing no information varies as per the amplitude of the signal containing information, at each instant.
- This can be well explained by the following figure.

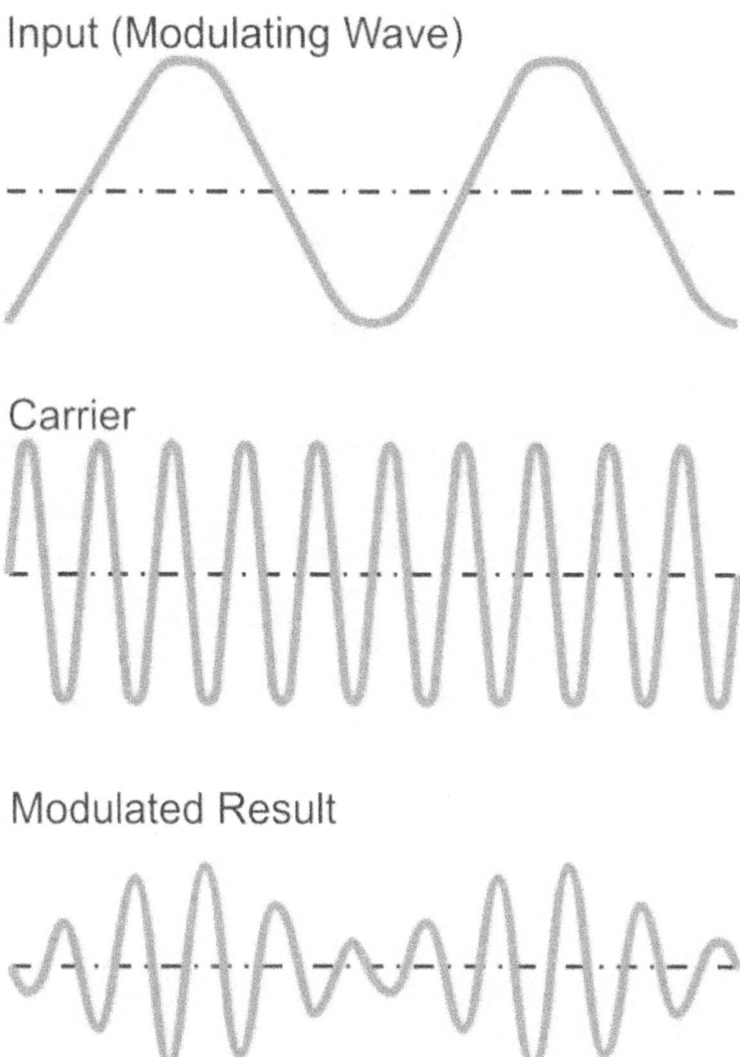

Figure 14: Amplitude Modulation

The figure shows the modulating wave, which is the message signal.

- The next one is the carrier wave, which is a high frequency signal and contains no information. While, the last one is the resultant modulated wave.
- Angle Modulation
- Angle modulation is further divided into frequency modulation and phase modulation.

    A. Frequency Modulation(FM)

- In amplitude modulation, the amplitude of the carrier signal varies. Whereas, in Frequency Modulation (FM), the frequency of the carrier signal varies in accordance with the instantaneous amplitude of the modulating signal.
- Hence, in frequency modulation, the amplitude and the phase of the carrier signal remains constant. This can be better understood by observing the following figure.

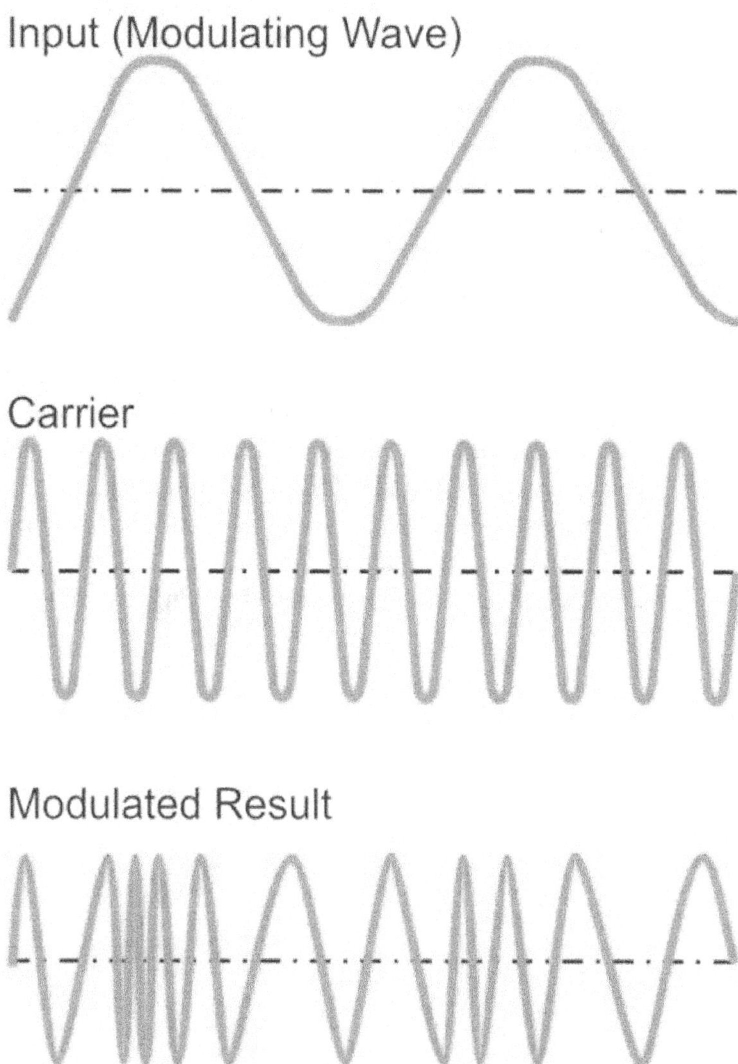

Figure 15: Frequency Modulation

- The frequency of the modulated wave increases, when the amplitude of the modulating or message signal increases.
- Similarly, the frequency of the modulated wave decreases, when the amplitude of the modulating signal decreases.
- Note that, the frequency of the modulated wave remains constant and it is equal to the frequency of the carrier signal, when the amplitude of the modulating signal is zero.

○ Phase Modulation(PM)

- In frequency modulation, the frequency of the carrier varies. Whereas, in Phase Modulation (PM), the phase of the carrier signal varies in accordance with the instantaneous amplitude of the modulating signal.
- So, in phase modulation, the amplitude and the frequency of the carrier signal remains constant.
- This can be better understood by observing the following figure.

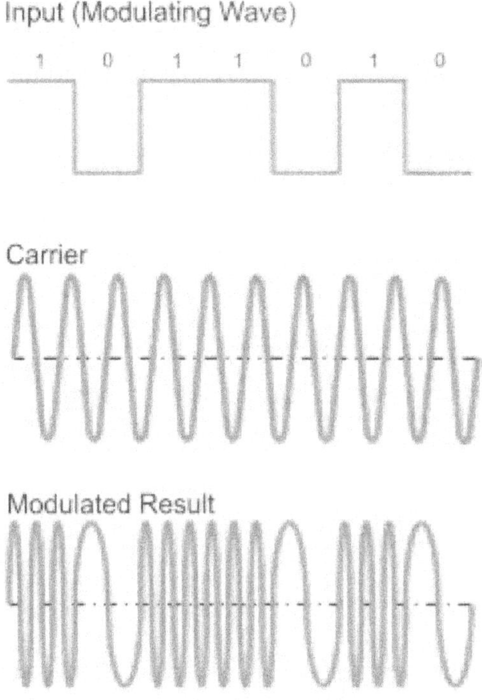

Figure 16: Phase Modulation

- The phase of the modulated wave has got infinite points, where the phase shift in a wave can take place.
- The instantaneous amplitude of the modulating signal changes the phase of the carrier signal.
- When the amplitude is positive, the phase changes in one direction and if the amplitude is negative, the phase changes in the opposite direction.

Analog Data, Digital Signal

- This process can be termed as digitization, which is done by Pulse Code Modulation (PCM). Hence, it is nothing but digital modulation.
- Here, Sampling and quantization are the important factors, so, Delta Modulation gives a better output than PCM.

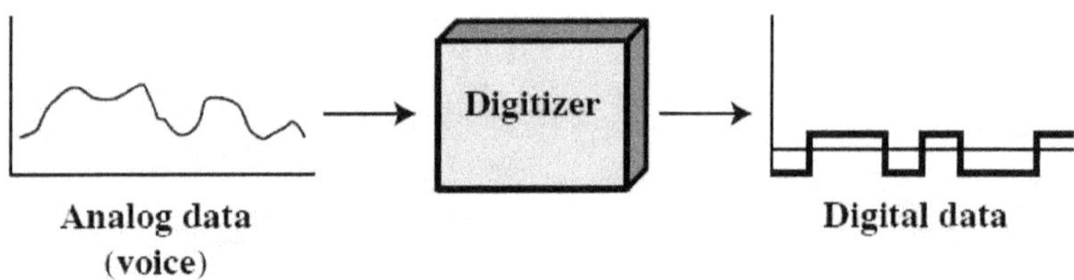

-

- Analog to digital conversion done using a codec (coder-decoder).

- Two principle codec techniques

A. Pulse Code Modulation
B. Delta modulation

A. Pulse Code Modulation

- A signal is pulse code modulated to convert its analog information into a binary sequence, i.e., 1s and 0s.
- The output of a PCM will resemble a binary sequence.
- The following figure shows an example of PCM output with respect to instantaneous values of a given sine wave.

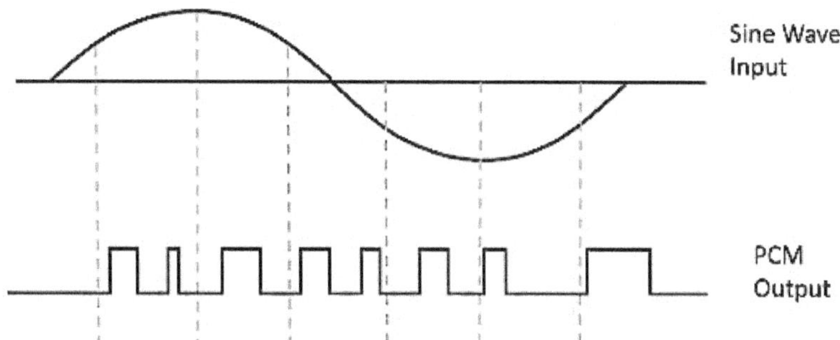

- Instead of a pulse train, PCM produces a series of numbers or digits, and hence this process is called as digital.
- Each one of these digits, though in binary code, represent the approximate amplitude of the signal sample at that instant.
- In Pulse Code Modulation, the message signal is represented by a sequence of coded pulses.
- This message signal is achieved by representing the signal in discrete form in both time and amplitude.

Spread Spectrum Techniques

- Mobile phone technology had a reincarnation from first generation analogue (using FDMA) to second generation digital (using TDMA).
- The next incarnation is from second generation digital TDMA to third generation packet (using CDMA).
- CDMA is a specific modulation technique of Spread-Spectrum technology.
- Third generation or 3G is more of a generic term to mean mobile networks with high bandwidth.

- In a conventional transmission system, the information is modulated with a carrier signal and then transmitted through a medium.
- When that transmitted, all the power of the signal is transmitted centered around a particular frequency. This frequency represents a specific channel and generally has a very narrow band.
- In spread-spectrum we spread the transmission power over the complete band as shown in figure.

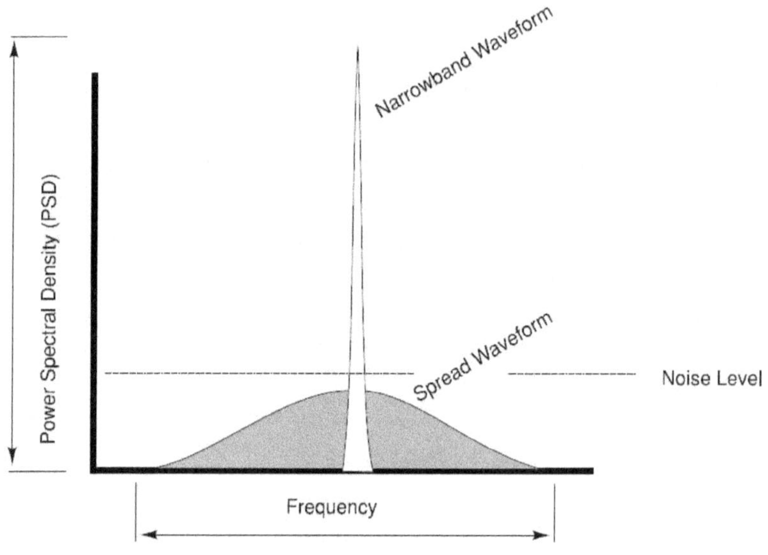

Figure 17: Spread Spectrum Technology

- In spread-spectrum the transmission signal bandwidth is much higher than the information bandwidth.
- There are numerous ways to cause a carrier to spread; however, all spread-spectrum systems can be viewed as two steps modulation processes.

- First, the data to be transmitted is modulated.
- Second, the carrier is modulated by the spreading code, causing it to spread out over a large bandwidth.

Different Spreading Techniques

- **Direct Sequence (DS):** DS spread spectrum is typically used to transmit digital information.
- A common practice in DS systems is to mix the digital information stream with a pseudo random code.
- **FrequencyHopping(FH):**Frequency hopping is a form of spreading in which the center frequency of a conventional carrier is altered many times within a fixed time period (like one second) in accordance with a pseudo-random list of channels.
- **Chirp:** The third spreading method employs a carrier that is swept over a range of frequencies.
- This method is called chirp spread spectrum and finds its primary application in ranging and radar systems.
- **Time Hopping:** The last spreading method is called time hopping. In a time-hopped signal, the carrier is on-off keyed by the pseudo-noise (PN) sequence resulting in a very low duty cycle.
- The speed of keying determines the amount of signal spreading.

- **Hybrid System:** A hybrid system combines the best points of two or more spread-spectrum systems. The performance of a hybrid system is usually better than can be obtained with a single spread-spectrum technique for the same cost.
- The most common hybrids combine both frequency-hopping and direct-sequence techniques.
- Amateurs and business community are currently authorized to use only two spreading techniques. These are frequency hopping and direct sequence techniques.
- Rest of the Spread-Spectrum technologies are classified and used by military and space sciences.

Explain Direct Sequence Spread Spectrum DSSS.

- Direct Sequence Spread Spectrum (DSSS) is often compared to a party, where many pairs are conversing, each in a different language.
- Each pair understands only one language and therefore, concentrates on his or her own conversation, ignoring the rest.
- A Hindi-speaking couple just homes on to Hindi, rejecting everything else as noise.
- Its analogous to DSSS is when pairs spread over the room conversing simultaneously, each pair in a different language. The key to DSSS is to be able to extract the desired signal while rejecting everything else as random noise.
- The analogy may not be exact, because a roomful of people all talking at once soon becomes very loud.
- In general, Spread-Spectrum communications is distinguished by three key elements:

1. The signal occupies a bandwidth much larger than what is necessary to send the information.
2. The bandwidth is spread by means of a code, which is independent of the data.
3. The receiver synchronizes to the code to recover the data. The use of an independent code and synchronous reception allows multiple users to access the same frequency band at the same time.

- In order to protect the signal, the code used is pseudo-random, which makes it appear random while being actually deterministic, which enables the receivers to reconstruct the code for synchronous detection. This pseudo-random code is also called pseudo-noise (PN).

- DSSS allows each station to transmit over the entire frequency all the time. DSSS also relaxes the assumption that colliding frames are totally garbled. Instead, it assumes that multiple signals add linearly.
- DSSS is commonly called Code Division Multiple Access or CDMA in short.
- Each station is assigned a unique m-bit code. This code is called the CDMA chip sequence. To transmit a 1 bit, the transmitting station sends its chip sequence, whereas to send 0, it sends the complement chip sequence.
- Example:

- Station – A
- Data: 0 0 (2 bit)
- Spreading code: 0 1 0 1

Spreading message: 0 1 0 1   0 1 0 1

```
Data   0000  0000
⊕ Code  0101  0101
       ──────────────
        0101  0101
```

- Station – B
- Data: 1 0 (2 bit)
- Spreading code: 0 0 1 1

Spreading message: 1 1 0 0   0 0 1 1

```
Data   1111  0000
⊕ Code  0011  0011
       ──────────────
        1100  0011
```

- Station – C
- Data: 1 1 (2 bit)
- Spreading code: 0 0 0 0

Spreading message: 1 1 1 1   1 1 1 1

```
Data   1111  1111
⊕ Code  0000  0000
       ──────────────
        1111  1111
```

- Combined all three spreading message
- Bit 0 then +1
- Bit 1 then -1

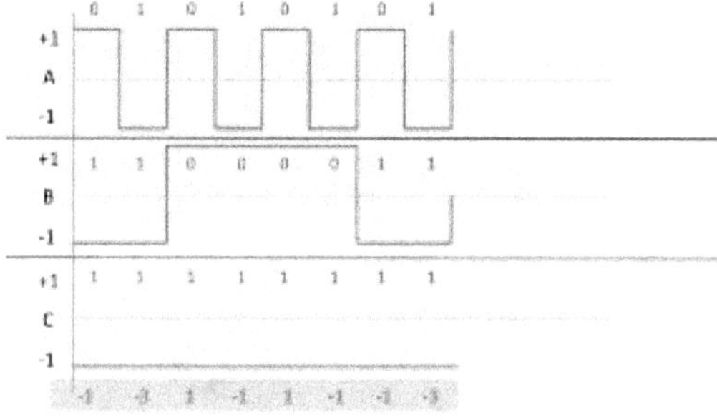

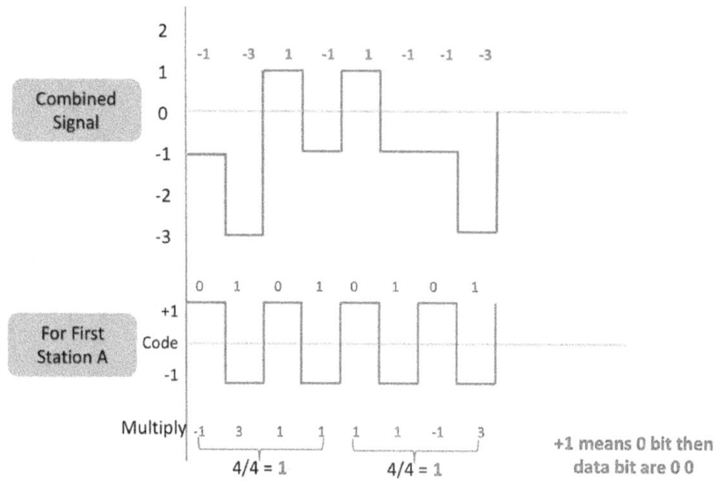

Error Control and Detection

- For reliable communication, errors must be detected and corrected.
- Data can be corrupted during transmission.
- Data-link layer uses some error control mechanism to ensure that frames (data bit streams) are transmitted with certain level of accuracy.
- Need to understand how errors is controlled and to know what types of errors may occur.
- Error detection and correction are implemented either at the data link layer or the transport layer of the OSI model.

Types of Errors

- There may be three types of errors:

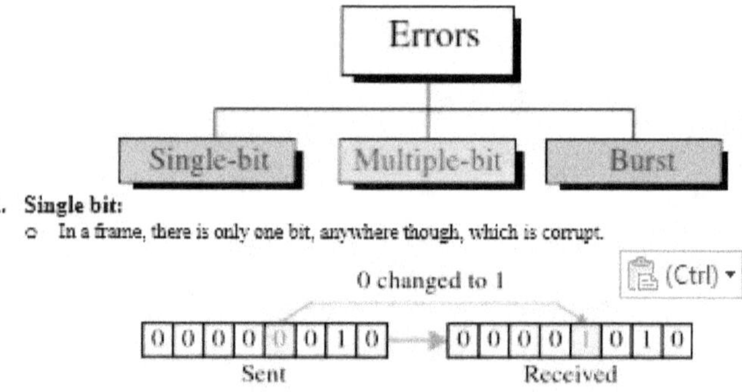

1. Single bit:
- o In a frame, there is only one bit, anywhere though, which is corrupt.

Types of Errors/ Single bit error

2. Multiple bit:
- o Frame is received with more than one bits in corrupted state.

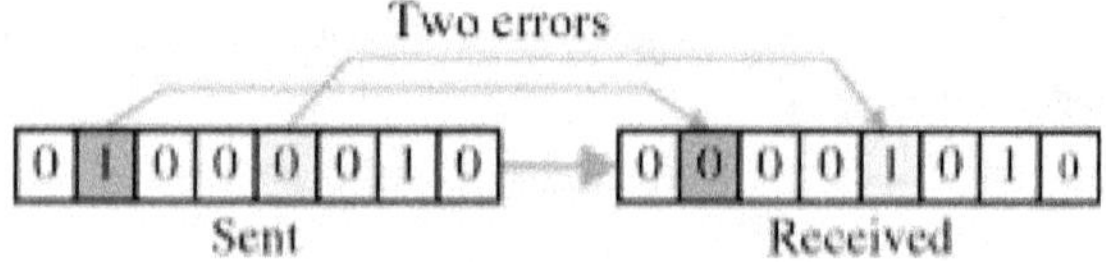

3. Burst:
- o Frame contains more than 1 consecutive bits corrupted.

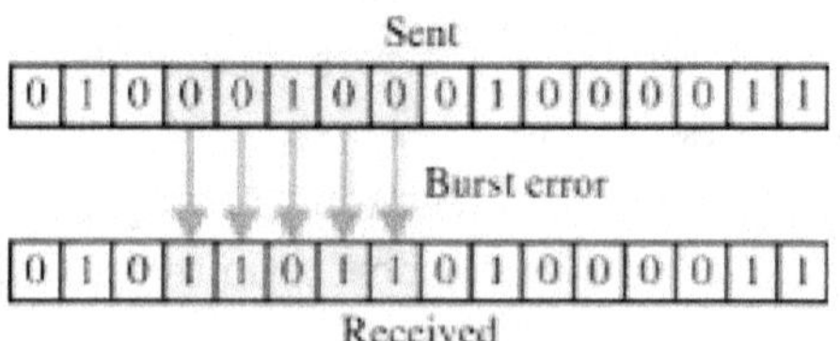

Error Detection Method

- Error detection means to decide whether the received data is correct or not without having a copy of the original message.
- Error detection uses the concept of redundancy, which means adding extra bits for detecting errors at the destination.

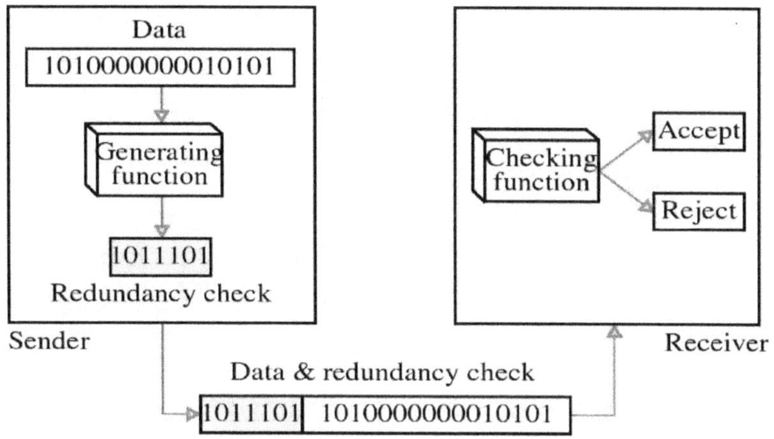

Figure 18: Redundancy

Detection Methods

1. Parity Check
2. Cyclic Redundancy check
3. Checksum

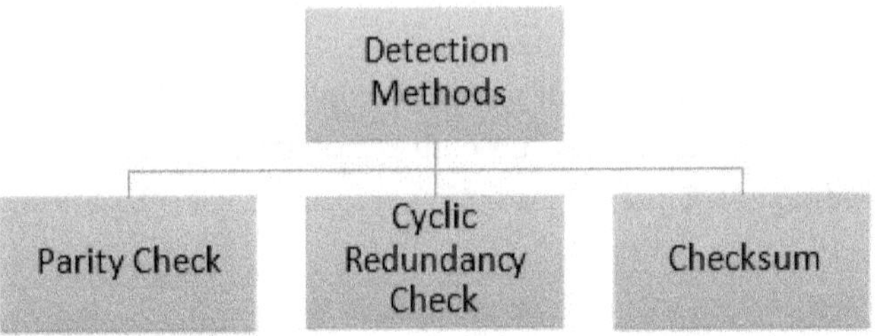

Figure 19: Detection Methods

Parity checks

- In this technique, a redundant bit called parity bit, is appended to every data unit so that the number of 1s in the unit including the parity becomes even.
- Blocks of data from the source are subjected to a check bit or Parity bit generator form, where a parity of 1 is added to the block if it contains an odd number of 1's and 0 is added if it contains an even number of 1's.
- At the receiving end the parity bit is computed from the received data bits and compared with the received parity bit.
- This scheme makes the total number of 1's even, that is why it is called even parity checking.

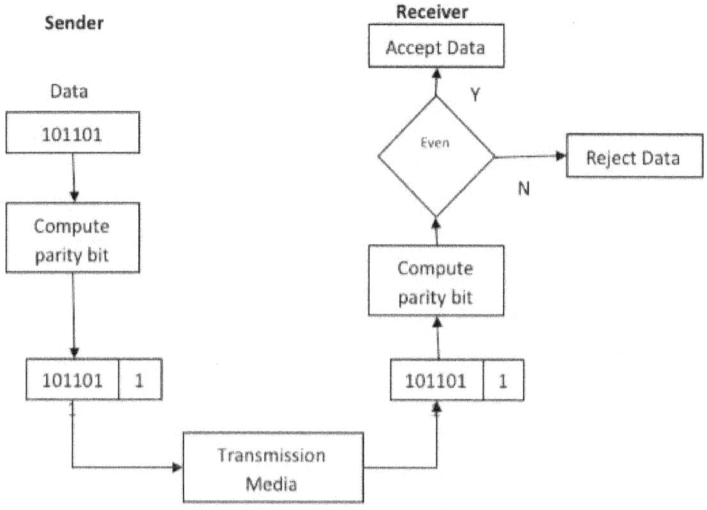

Figure 20: Even parity checking scheme

Performance

- A receiver can detect all single bit errors in each code word.
- Errors in more than one bit cannot be detected.

Two-dimension Parity Check

- Performance can be improved by using two-dimensional parity check, which organizes the block of bits in the form of a table.
- Parity check bits are calculated for each row, which is equivalent to a simple parity check bit.
- Parity check bits are also calculated for all columns then both are sent along with the data.
- At the receiving end these are compared with the parity bits calculated on the received data.

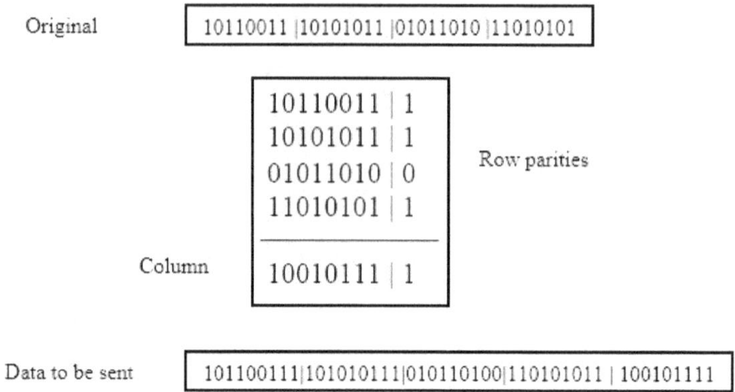

Figure 21: Two-Dimensional parity check

Performance

- Two- Dimension Parity Checking increases the likelihood of detecting burst errors.
- 2-D Parity check of n bits can detect a burst error of n bits.
- A burst error of more than n bits is also detected by 2-D Parity check with a high-probability.
- If two bits in one data unit are damaged and two bits in exactly same position in another data unit are also damaged, the 2-D Parity check checker will not detect an error.

Checksum

- Here, the data is divided into k segments each of m bits.
- In the sender's end the segments are added using 1's complement arithmetic to get the sum.
- The sum is complemented to get the checksum.
- The checksum segment is sent along with the data segments.

- At the receiver's end, all received segments are added using 1's complement arithmetic to get the sum. The sum is complemented.
- If the result is zero, the received data is accepted; otherwise discarded.

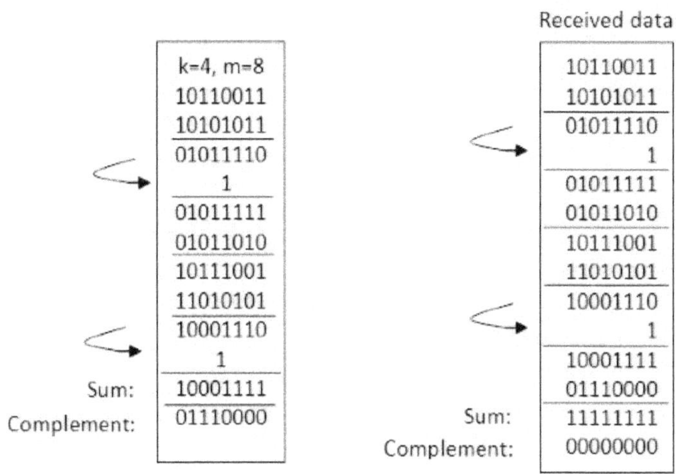

Figure 22: Checksum

Performance

- The checksum detects all errors involving an odd number of bits.
- It also detects most errors involving even number of bits.

Cyclic Redundancy Checks (CRC)

- CRC is the most powerful and easy to implement technique.
- CRC is based on binary division.
- In CRC, a sequence of redundant bits, are appended to the end of data unit so that the resulting data unit becomes exactly

divisible by a second, predetermined binary number.

- At the destination, the incoming data unit is divided by the same number.
- If at this step there is no remainder, the data unit is assumed to be correct and is therefore accepted.
- A remainder indicates that the data unit has been damaged in transit and therefore must be rejected.
- The binary number, which is (r+1) bit in length, can also be considered as the coefficients of a polynomial, called Generator Polynomial.

Performance

- CRC is a very effective error detection technique.
- If the divisor is chosen according to the previously mentioned rules, its performance can be summarized as follows
- CRC can detect all single-bit errors
- CRC can detect all double-bit errors (three 1's)
- CRC can detect any odd number of errors (X+1)
- CRC can detect all burst errors of less than the degree of the polynomial.

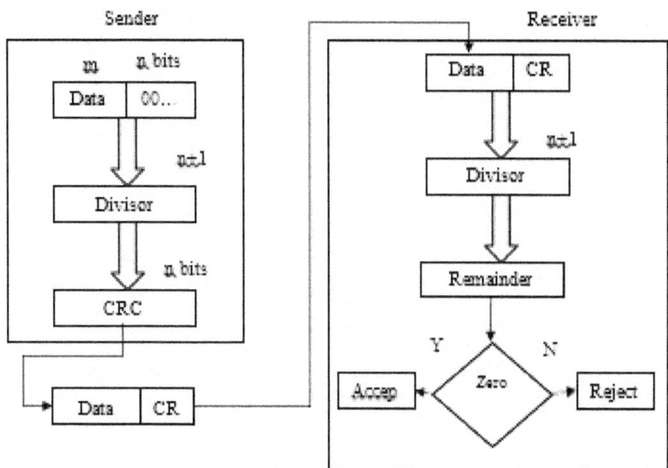

Figure 23: Basic scheme for Cyclic Redundancy Check

Frame   : 1 1 0 1 0 1 1 0 1 1
Generator: 1 0 0 1 1
Message after appending 4 zero bits: 1 1 0 1 0 1 1 0 0 0 0

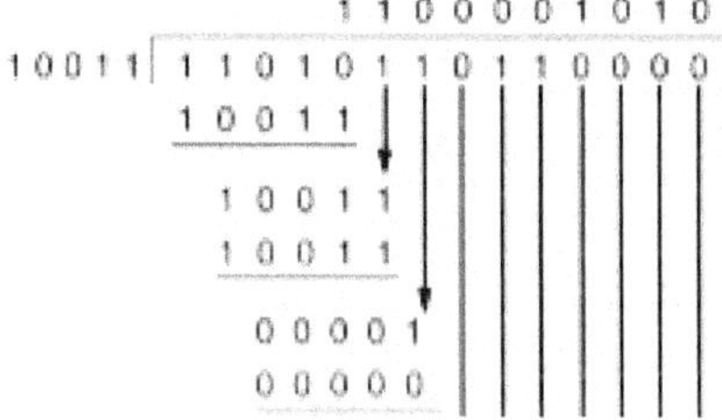

93

```
Frame     :  1 1 0 1 0 1 1 0 1 1
Generator:  1 0 0 1 1
Message after appending 4 zero bits:  1 1 0 1 0 1 1 0 0 0 0

                              1 1 0 0 0 0 1 0 1 0
              10011| 1 1 0 1 0 1 1 0 1 1 0 0 0 0

                              1 0 1 0 0
                              1 0 0 1 1

                                  0 1 1 1 0
                                  0 0 0 0 0         — Remainder
                                    1 1 1 0
```

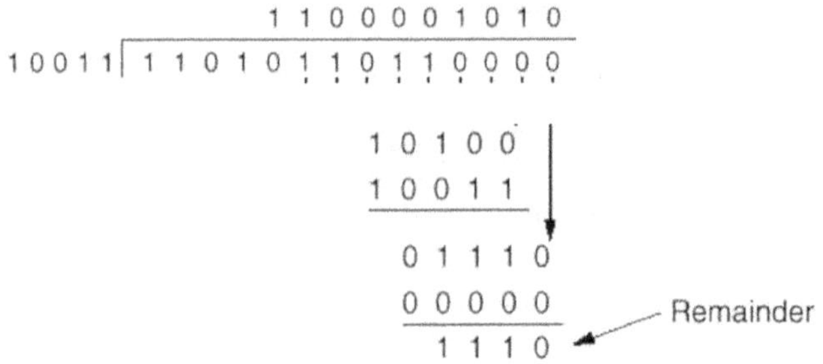

Transmitted frame: 1 1 0 1 0 1 1 0 1 1 1 1 1 0

Block Error Correction Code

Hamming Code:

- Hamming code is a set of error-correction codes that can be used to detect and correct the errors that can occur when the data is moved or stored from the sender to the receiver.
- Redundant bits are extra binary bits that are generated and added to the carrying bits of data transfer.
- The number of redundant bits can be calculated by:

$$?^{?} > ? + ? + ?$$

- where, r = redundant bit, m = data bit
- Example, the number of data bits is 7, then the number of redundant bits can be calculated using:

$$?^{?} > ? + ? + ?$$

- Thus, the number of redundant bits= 4
- **Step-1**

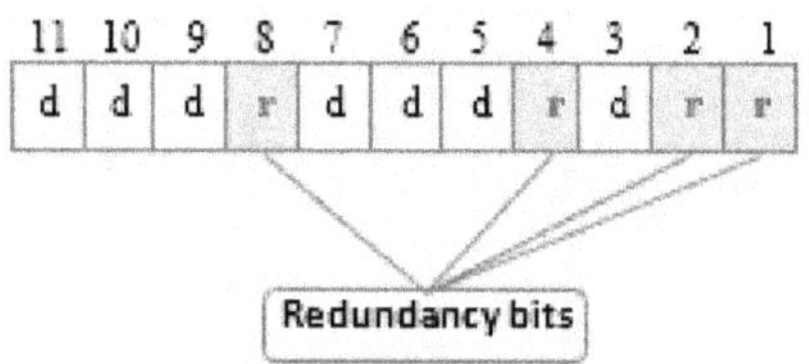

- Step-2

r1 will take care of these bits
1011   1001   0111   0101   0011   0001
11   9   7   5   3   1
d   d   d   r8   d   d   d   r4   d   r2   r1

r2 will take care of these bits
1011 1010   0111 0110   0011 0010
11   10   7   6   3   2
d   d   d   r8   d   d   d   r4   d   r2   r1

- Step:3

r4 will take care of these bits
0111 0110 0101 0100
7   6   5   4
d   d   d   r8   d   d   d   r4   d   r2   r1

r8 will take care of these bits
1011 1010 1001 1000
11   10   9   8
d   d   d   r8   d   d   d   r4   d   r2   r1

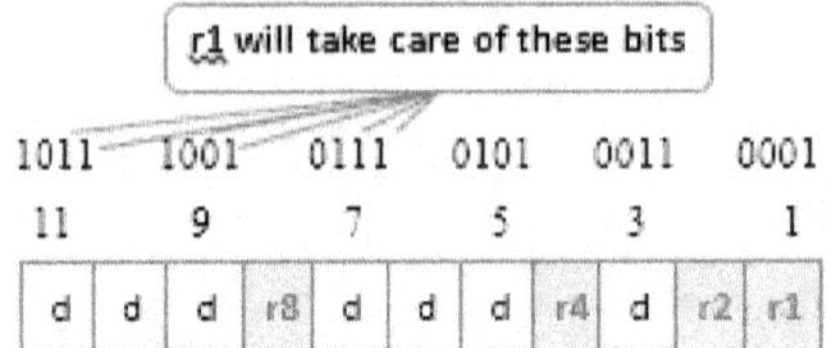

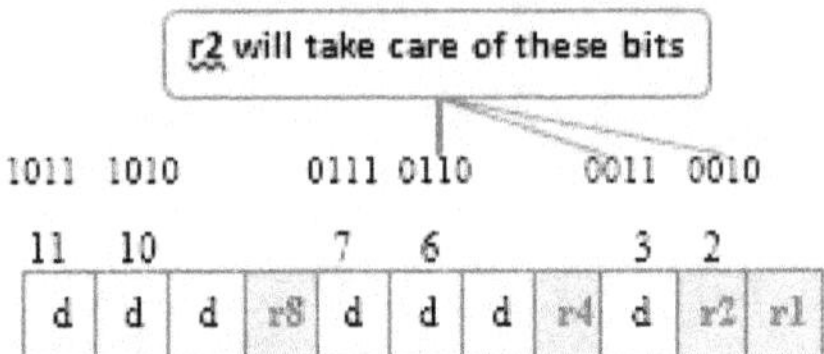

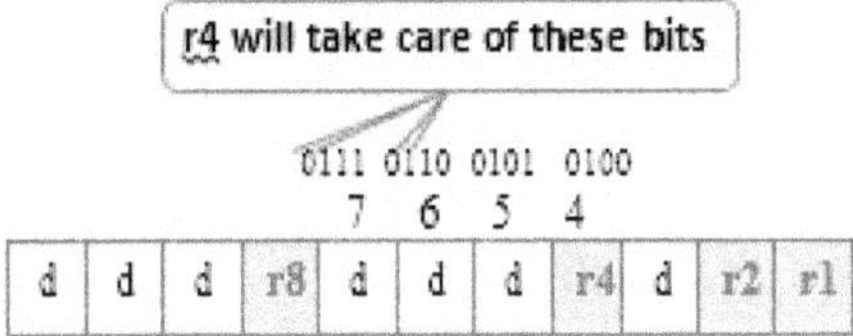

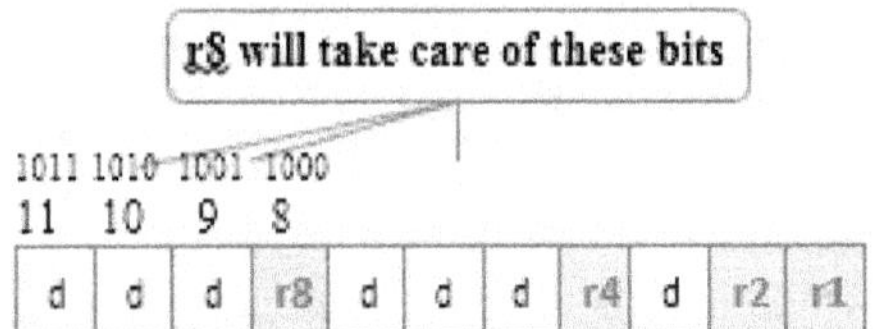

Example

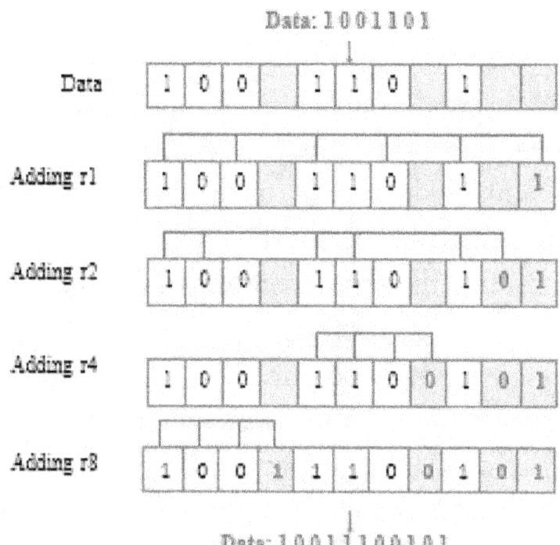

- Error in transmission

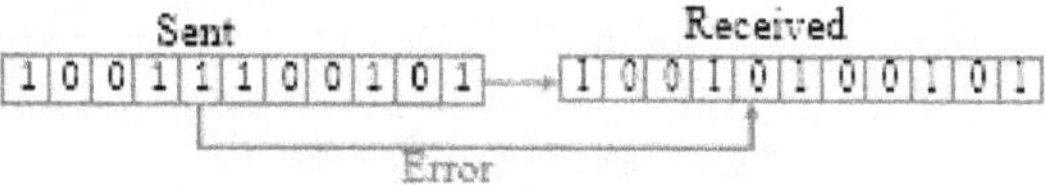

- Error bit detection

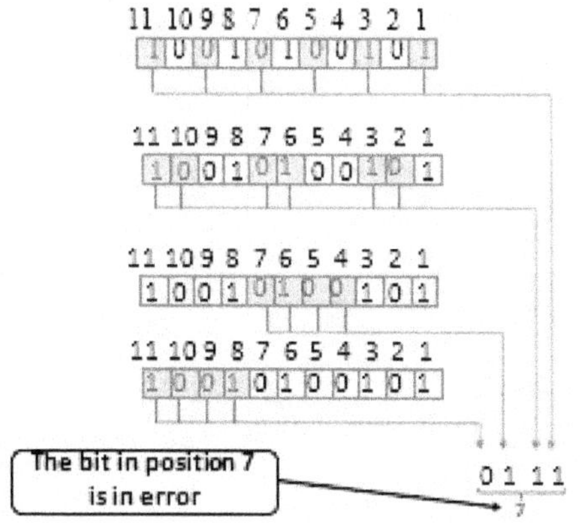

Automatic Repeat Request

- Automatic repeat request (ARQ), also known as automatic repeat query, is an error- control method for data transmission that uses acknowledgements and timeouts to achieve reliable data transmission over an unreliable service.
- If the sender does not receive an acknowledgment before the timeout, then re-transmits the frame/packet until the sender receives an acknowledgment.
- The types of ARQ protocols include Stop-and-wait ARQ, Go-Back-N ARQ, and Selective Repeat ARQ / Selective Reject.
- These protocols reside in the Data Link or Transport Layers of the OSI model.

List and discuss at least seven functions where CDMA is different from GSM.

Functions	GSM	CDMA(IS-95)
Frequency	900MHz; 1800MHz;1900MHz	800MHz;1900MHz
Channel Bandwidth	Total 25 MHz bandwidth with 200 KHz per channels, 8 timeslots per channel with frequency hopping.	Total 12MHz with 1.25 MHzfor the spread spectrum.
Voice Codec	13Kbits/second	8Kbits/second or 13Kbps
Data bit rate	9.6 Kbits/second or expandable	9.6Kbits
SMS	160 characters of text supports	120 characters
SIM Card	Yes	No
Multipath	Causes interference and destruction to service	Used as an advantage
Radio Interface	TDMA	CDMA
Handoff	Hard	Soft
System Capacity	Fixed and limited	Flexible and higher than GSM

Discuss 3G versus Wi-Fi

Functions	3G	Wi-Fi
Radio Interface	Uses spread spectrum as the modulation technique.	Uses spread spectrum as the modulation technique.
Genesis	Evolved from voice network where QoS is a critical success factor.	Evolved from data network where QoS is not a critical success factor.
Bandwidth	It supports broadband data service of up to 2Mbps.	Wi-Fi supports broadband data service of up to 54Mbps.
Status of standards	For 3G, there is a relatively small family of internationally sanctioned standards, collectively referred to as IMT-2000.	It is one of the families of continuously evolving 802.11x wireless standards that are under development.
Access Technologies	Access or edge-network facility. The wireless link is from the end-user device to the cell base station, which may be at a distance of up to a few kilometers.	Access or edge-network facility. The wireless link is a few hundred feet from the end-user device to the base station.
Business models/deployment are different	Service providers own and manage the infrastructure. End customers typically have a monthly service contract with the 3G service provider to use the network.	Users' organization owns the infrastructure. Following the initial investment, the usage of the network does not involve an access fee.
Roaming	It will offer well-coordinated continuous and ubiquitous coverage.	Seamless ubiquitous roamingover Wi-Fi cannot be guaranteed as network growth is unorganized.

What is 3G? List applications on 3G

- The term 3G internet refers to the third generation of mobile phone standards, as set by the International Telecommunications Union (ITU).
- 3G technologies allow mobile operators to offer more service options to their users, including mobile broadband.
- 3G broadband offers greater flexibility and services by making more efficient use of mobile bandwidth than its predecessor 2G.
- Devices in 3G can work in multiple ways. They can run in a tunneling mode or in an application mode.
- **In tunneling mode**, the device works more as a pass through device or a modem. In this mode, the mobile phone is connected to another device like a laptop and functions as a wireless media interface. The intelligence of the phone is not used, only the communication interface of the phone is used.
- **In an application mode**, applications run on the phone itself. A 3G mobile phone will support, SMS, WAP, Java, etc. (MExE classmark 3). A MExE classmark 3 mobile device will have an execution environment that will allow application development for the client device.

Applications on 3G

- In 3G, there will be different types of client applications: Local, Occasionally connected, Online and Real-time.
- Games, cartoons and similar applications are examples of local applications. These applications can be downloaded over the air and used offline.
- In an occasionally connected computing (OCC) environment, the user will connect to the network occasionally. Downloading and uploading of emails are the best examples of OCC.

- Online applications will be the corporate applications. Examples of such applications will be online order booking or updating of inventory status.
- Real-time applications could be real-time stock updates or applications for law-enforcement agents for real-time tracking or navigational systems.
- Few 3G specific applications are:

  - **Virtual Home Environment (VHE)** – Virtual Home Environment can be defined as a concept where an environment is created in a foreign network (or home network outside the home environment).
  - So, that the mobile users can experience the same computing experience as they have in their home or corporate computing environment while they are mobile and roaming.
  - **Personal Communication Networks (PCN)** – These are digital telephone networking infrastructures, which supports personal numbering, individual service selection, and moves towards unified billing and call anytime, anywhere through wireless digital telephony.
  - **Universal Subscriber Identity Module (USIM)** – This is the smart card for third generation mobile phones. A SIM card in the mobile phone offers portability, security and individuality.
  - **Audio/Video**– Third generation applications will be used to download music, multimedia, news, etc.
  - VIP
  - **Electronic Agents** – Electronic agents are defined as "mobile programs that go places in the network to carry out their owners' instructions. They can be thought of as extensions of the people who dispatch them."
  - Dwnloading f Sftware and Cntent
  - **ENUM** – ENUM is a protocol that is emerging from work of Internet Engineering Task Force's (IETF's) Telephone Number Mapping working group.

3

GSM & GPRS

Multiplexing Techniques.

Frequency Division Multiple Access (FDMA)

- It is one of the most common multiplexing procedures. FDMA is a channel access technique found in multiple-access protocols as a channelization protocol.
- FDMA permits individual allocation of single or multiple frequency bands, or channels to the users.
- FDMA permits multiple users to simultaneously access a transmission system.
- In FDMA, every user shares the frequency channel or satellite transponder simultaneously; however, every user transmits at single frequency.
- FDMA is compatible with both digital and analog signals.
- FDMA demands highly efficient filters in the radio hardware, contrary to CDMA and TDMA.
- FDMA is devoid of timing issues that exist in TDMA.
- As a result of the frequency filtering, FDMA is not prone to the near-far problem that exists in CDMA.
- All users transmit and receive at different frequencies because every user receives an individual frequency slot.

- One disadvantage of FDMA is crosstalk, which can cause interference between frequencies and interrupt the transmission.

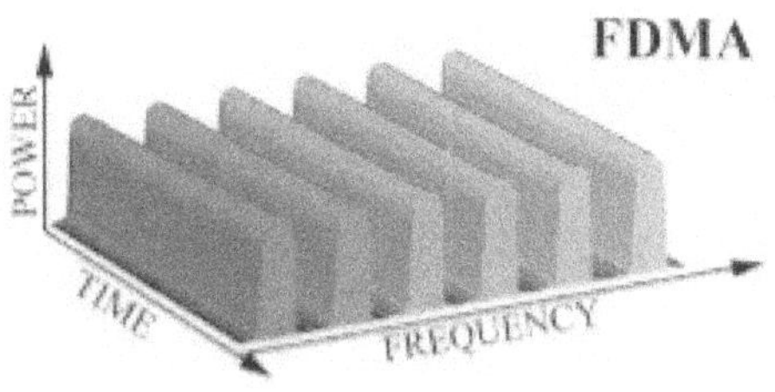

Figure 1: Frequency Division Multiple Access

Space Division Multiple Access (SDMA)

- SDMA utilizes the spatial separation of the users in order to optimize the use of the frequency spectrum.
- A primitive form of SDMA is when the same frequency is reused in different cells in a cellular wireless network.
- The radiated power of each user is controlled by Space division multiple access.
- SDMA serves different users by using spot beam antenna. These areas may be served by the same frequency or different frequencies.
- However for limited co-channel interference it is required that the cells are sufficiently separated. This limits the number of cells a region can be divided into and hence limits the frequency re-use factor. A more advanced approach can further increase the capacity of the network. This technique would enable frequency re-use within the cell. In a practical cellular environment it is improbable to have just one transmitter fall within the receiver beam width. Therefore it becomes imperative to use other multiple access techniques in conjunction with

SDMA.

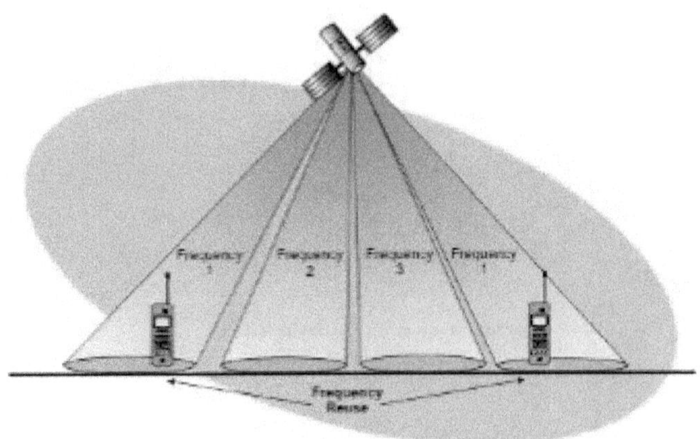

Figure 2: Space Division Multiple Access

- When different areas are covered by the antenna beam, frequency can be re-used, in which case TDMA or CDMA is employed, for different frequencies FDMA can be used.

Time Division Multiple Access (TDMA)

- It is a multiplexing technique where multiple channels are multiplexed over time.
- In TDMA, several users share the same frequency channel of higher bandwidth by dividing the signal into different time slots.
- Users transmit their data using their own respective time slots in rapid succession; to synchronize, the transmitter and the receiver need to synchronize using a global clock.
- It is divided into two types:-

Fixed TDMA

- In this, connections between time slots in each frame and data streams assigned to a user remain static and switched only when large variations in traffic are required.
- In this variant, the slot sizes are fixed at T/N (T is time in seconds and N is the number of users).

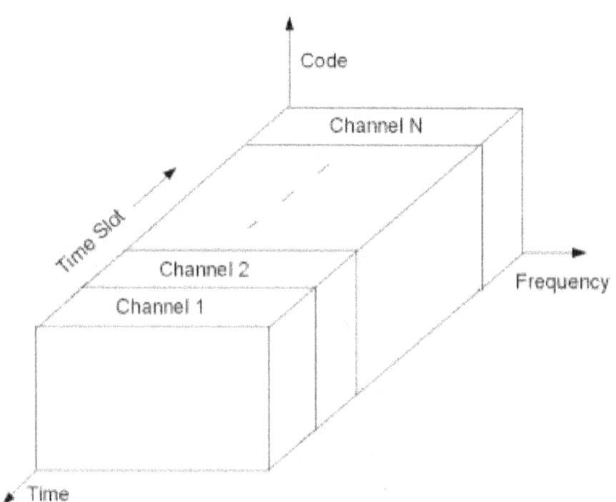

Figure 3: Time Division Multiple Access

Dynamic TDMA

- In this, a scheduling algorithm is used to dynamically reserve a variable number of time slots in each frame to variable bit-rate data streams.
- This reservation algorithm is based on the traffic demand of each data stream.

Code Division Multiple Access (CDMA)

- Short for Code-Division Multiple Access, a digital cellular technology that uses spread-spectrum techniques. It is a broadband system.
- CDMA uses spread spectrum technique where each subscriber uses the whole system bandwidth.

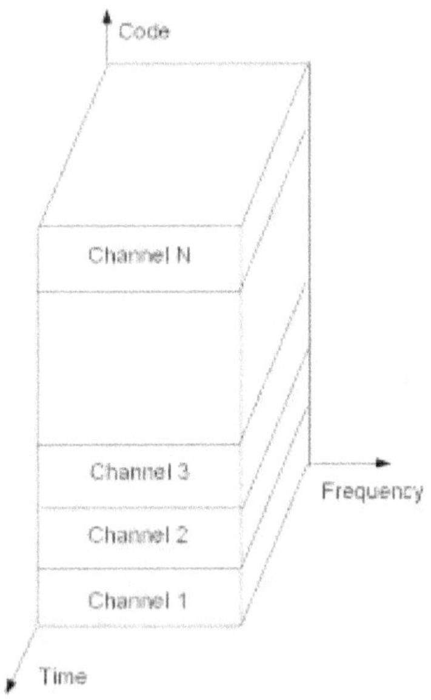

Figure 4: Code Division Multiple Access

- Unlike competing systems, such as GSM, that use TDMA, CDMA does not assign a specific frequency to each user.
- Instead, every channel uses the full available spectrum. Individual conversations are encoded with a pseudo-random digital sequence.

- CDMA consistently provides better capacity for voice and data communications than other commercial mobile technologies, allowing more subscribers to connect at any given time, and it is the common platform on which 3G technologies are built.
- For example, CDMA is a military technology first used during World War II by English allies to foil German attempts at jamming transmissions.
- Unlike the FDMA or TDMA where a frequency or time slot is assigned exclusively to a subscriber, in CDMA all subscribers in a cell use the same frequency band simultaneously.
- To separate the signals, each subscriber is assigned an orthogonal code called "chip".

Principles of Cellular Network

- Cellular technology is the basis for mobile wireless communications and supports users in locations that are not easily served by wired networks.
- Cellular radio is a technique that was developed to increase the capacity available for mobile radio telephone service.
- It is an underlying technology for mobile phones, personal communication systems, wireless networking, etc.
- This technology is developed for a mobile radio telephone to replace high power transmitter/receiver systems.
- Cellular network uses lower power, shorter range and more transmitters for data transmission.
- A cellular network divides any given area into cells where a mobile unit in each cell communicates with a base station.
- The main aim of the cellular network design is to be able to increase the capacity of the channel.
- For Example, to handle as many calls as possible in a given bandwidth with a sufficient level of quality of service.

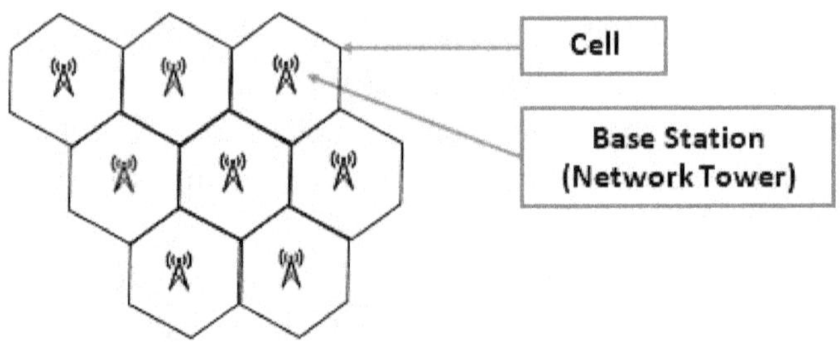

Figure 5: Cell and Base Station

Cell Structure

- The coverage area of cellular networks divided into cells, each cell having its own antenna for transmitting the signals.
- Each cell has its own frequencies.
- Though in reality, these cells could be of any shape, for proper modeling purposes these are modeled as hexagons.

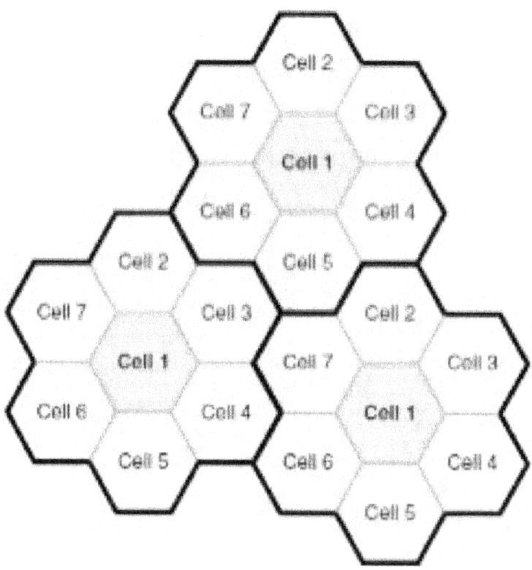

Figure 6: Cell Structure

- A hexagon cell shape is highly recommended for its easy coverage and calculations. It offers the following advantages –

  - Provides equidistant antennas.
  - Distance from center to vertex equals length of side.

Frequency Reuse

- To serve hundreds of thousands of users, the frequency must be reused and this is done through cells.
- The area to be covered and subdivided into radio zones or cells.

- Base station positioned at the center of the cell.
- Data communication in cellular networks served by its base station transmitter, receiver, and its control unit.
- When moving from one cell to another during an ongoing conversation, an automatic channel change occurs.
- This phenomenon is called handover. Handover maintains an active speech and data connection over cell boundaries.
- The regular repetition of frequencies in cells results in a clustering of cells.
- The clusters generated in this way can consume the whole frequency band.

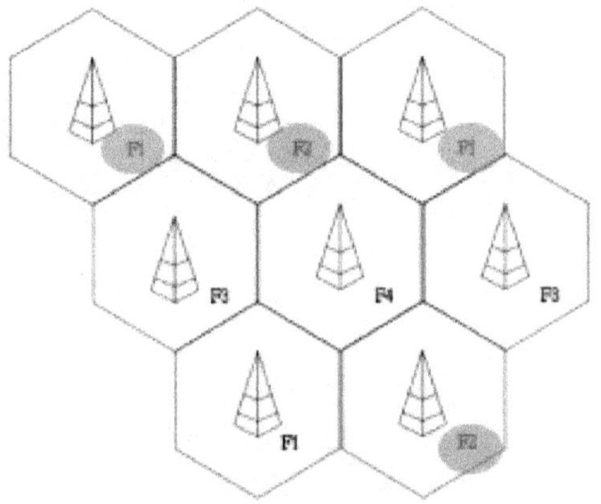

Figure 7: Frequency Reuse

Cell Cluster

- Each cell ? receives a subset of frequencies ??? from the entire set assigned to the respective mobile network.

- To avoid any co-channel interference two neighboring cells never uses the same frequencies.
- Only at a distance of ? (known as frequency reuse distance), the same frequency from the set ??? can be reused.

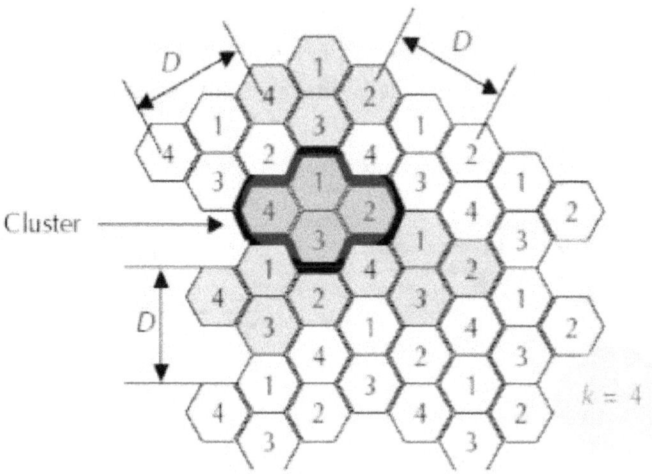

Figure 8: Cell Cluster

- Cells with distance ? from cell ?, can be assigned one or all the frequencies from the set ??? belonging to cell ?.
- The size of a cluster defined by ?, the number of cells in the cluster.
- It also defines the frequency reuse distance ?. The figure shows an example of cluster size of 4.

GSM Specification

- Uses a combination of FDMA (Frequency Division Multiple Access) and TDMA (Time Division Multiple Access).
- Allocation of 50 MHz (890–915 MHz and 935–960 MHz) bandwidth in the 900 MHz frequency band and using FDMA further divided into 124 (125 channels, 1 not used) channels each with a carrier bandwidth of 200 KHz.
- Using TDMA, each of the above mentioned channels is then further divided into 8 time slots
- So, with the combination of FDMA and TDMA, a maximum of992 channels for transmit and receive can be realized.

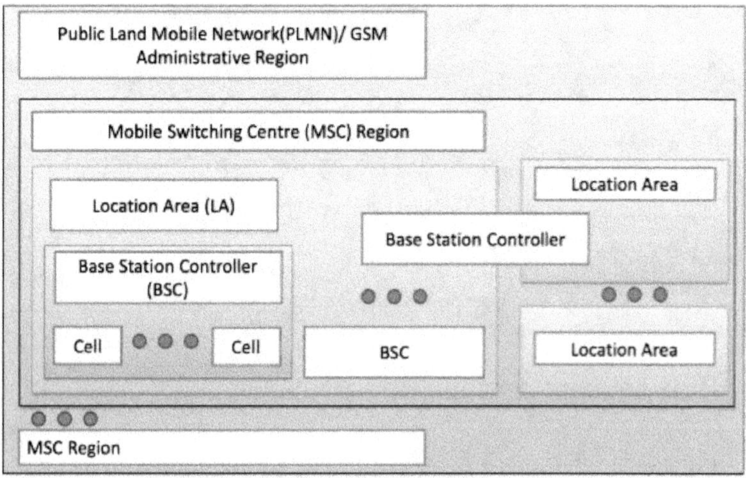

Figure 9: GSM System Hierarchy

- It consists of the minimum one administrative region assigned to one Mobile Switching Centre (MSC).
- An administrative region is commonly known as Public Land Mobile Network (PLMN).

- Each administrative region subdivided into one or many Location Area (LA).
- One LA consists of many cell groups and each cell group assigned to one Base Station Controller (BSC).
- For each LA, there will be at least one BSC while cells in one BSC can belong to different LA.

GSM Architecture

- In System, It consists at the minimum one administrative region assigned to one MSC (Mobile Switching Centre).
- Administrative region is commonly known as PLMN (Public Land Mobile Network).
- Each administrative region is subdivided into one or many Location Area (LA).
- One LA consists of many cell groups and each cell group is assigned to one BSC (Base Station Controller).
- For each LA, there will be at least one BSC while cells in one BSC can belong to different LAs.

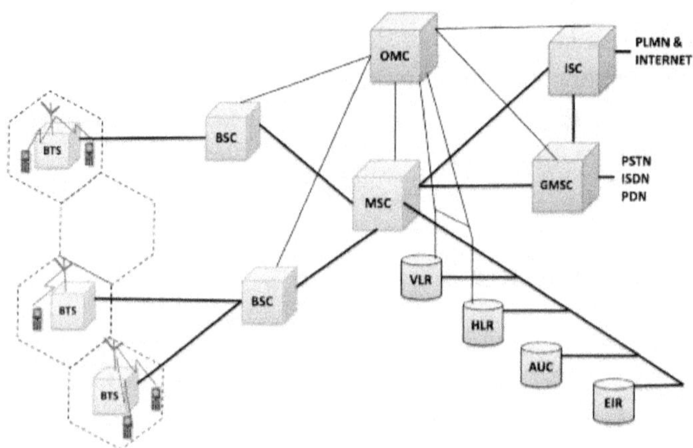

Figure 10: GSM Architecture

AUC – Authentication Center	ISDN – Integrated System Digital Network
BSC – Base Station Controller	MS – Mobile Station
BTS – Base Transceiver Station	MSC – Mobile Switching Center
EIR – Equipment Identity Register	OMC – Operation and Maintenance Center
GMSC – Gateway MSC	PDN – Packet Data Network
HLR – Home Location Register	PLMN – Public Land Mobile Network
ISC – International Switching Center	PSTN – Public Switched Telephone Network
VLR – Visitor Location Register	

- Cells are formed by the radio areas covered by a **BTS** (Base Transceiver Station). Several BTSs are controlled by one BSC.
- Traffic from the **MS** (Mobile Station) is routed through **MSC**. Calls originating from or terminating in a fixed network or other mobile networks is handled by the **GMSC** (Gateway MSC)

- For all subscribers registered with a cellular network operator, permanent data such as the service profile is stored in the Home Location Register (**HLR**). The data relate to the following information:-

  - Authentication information like IMSI.
  - Identification information like name, address, etc., of the subscriber.
  - Identification information like MSISDN, etc.
  - Billing information like prepaid or postpaid customer.
  - Operator select denial of service to a subscriber.
  - Handling of supplementary services like for CFU (Call Forwarding Unconditional), CFB (Call Forwarding Busy), CFNR (Call Forwarding Not Reachable) or CFNA (Call Forwarding Not Answered)
  - Storage of SMS Service Center (SC) number in case the mobile is not connectable so that whenever the mobile is connectable, a paging signal is sent to the SC
  - Provisioning information like whether long distance and international calls allowed or not.
  - Provisioning information like whether roaming is enabled or not
  - Information related to auxiliary services like Voice mail, data, fax services, etc.
  - Information related to auxiliary services like CLI (Caller Line Identification), etc.
  - Information related to supplementary services for call routing. In GSM network, one can customize the personal profile to the extent that while the subscriber is roaming in a foreign PLMN, incoming calls can be barred. Also, outgoing international calls can be barred, etc.
  - Some variable information like pointer to the VLR, location area of the subscriber, Power OFF status of the handset, etc.

- The GSM technical specifications define different entities that form the GSM network by defining their functions and interface requirements. The GSM network can be divided into 5 main groups:-
- **The Mobile Station (MS):** This includes the Mobile Equipment (ME) and the Subscriber Identity Module (SIM).
- **The Base Station Subsystem (BSS):** This includes the Base Transceiver Station (BTS) and the Base Station Controller (BSC).
- **The Network and Switching Subsystem (NSS):** This includes Mobile Switching Center (MSC), Home Location Register (HLR), Visitor Location Register (VLR), Equipment Identity Register (EIR), and the Authentication Center (AUC).
- **The Operation and Support Subsystem (OSS):** This includes the Operation and Maintenance Center (OMC).
- The data infrastructure that includes Public Switched Telephone Network (PSTN), Integrated System Digital Network (ISDN), and the Public Data Network (PDN)

Entities in GSM

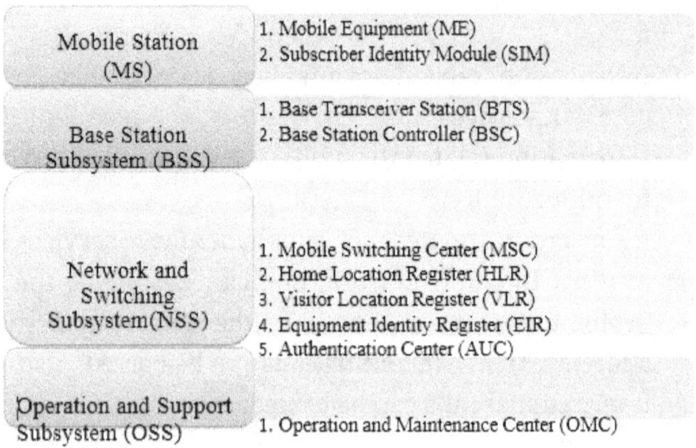

Figure 11: Entity in GSM

Mobile Station(MS)

- Mobile Station (MS) consists of two main elements:

  - Mobile equipment or mobile device (that is the phone without the SIM card)
  - Subscriber Identity Module (SIM)

- Terminals distinguished principally by their power and application.
- SIM is installed in every GSM phone and identifies the terminal.
- SIM cards used in GSM phones are smart processor cards possess a processor and a small memory.
- SIM card contains the International Mobile Subscriber Identity (IMSI) used to identify the subscriber to the system, a secret key for authentication, and other security information.

Base Station Subsystem (BSS)

- Base Station Subsystem (BSS) connects the Mobile Station and the Network and Switching Subsystem (NSS)
- It is in charge of the transmission and reception for the last mile.
- BSS divided into two parts:

  1. Base Transceiver Station (BTS) or Base Station
  2. Base Station Controller (BSC)

- Base Transceiver Station corresponds to the transceivers and antennas used in each cell of the network.
- BTS usually placed in the center of a cell and its transmitting power defines the size of a cell.

- BTS holds the radio transmitter and the receivers that define a cell and handles the radio-link protocols with the Mobile Station.

- Each BTS has between 1 and 16 transceivers depending on the density of users in the cell.
- Base Station Controller is the connection between the BTS and the Mobile service Switching Center (MSC) and manages the radio resources for one or more BTSs.
- BSC handles:

  - Handovers process.
  - Radio-channel setup.
  - Control of radio frequency power levels of the BTSs.
  - Exchange function, and frequency hopping.

Network and Switching Subsystem (NSS)

- A central component of the Network Subsystem is the Mobile Switching Center (MSC).
- Signaling between functional entities in the Network Subsystem uses Signaling System Number 7 (SS7).
- MSC together with Home Location Register (HLR) and Visitor Location Register (VLR) databases, provide the call-routing and roaming capabilities of GSM.
- **Mobile Switching Centre - MSC** does the following functions:
- It acts like a typical switching node for mobile subscribers of the same network (connection between mobile phone to mobile phone within the same network).
- It acts like a typical switching node for the PSTN fixed telephone (connection between mobile phone to fixed phone).
- It acts like a typical switching node for Integrated Service digital Network - ISDN.
- It provides all functionality needed to handle a mobile subscriber, such as registration, authentication, location updating, handovers and call routing.
- It includes databases to store information to manage the mobility of a roaming subscriber.

- MSC together with Home Location Register (HLR) and Visitor Location Register (VLR) databases, provide the call-routing and roaming capabilities of GSM.
- HLR contains all the administrative information of each subscriber registered in the corresponding GSM network.
- Location of the mobile is typically in the form of the signaling address of the VLR associated with the mobile station.
- HLR is always fixed and stored in the home network, whereas the VLR logically moves with the subscriber.
- VLR is similar to a cache, whereas HLR is the persistent storage.
- VLR contains selected administrative information borrowed from the HLR, necessary for call control and provisioning of the subscribed services.
- When a subscriber enters the covering area of a new MSC, the VLR associated with this MSC can request information about the new subscriber from its corresponding HLR in the home network.
- There is a component called Gateway MSC (GMSC) that associated with the MSC.
- GMSC is the interface between the mobile cellular network and the PSTN and also is in charge of routing calls from the fixed network towards a GSM user and vice versa.
- GMSC often implemented in the same node as the MSC.
- GIWU (GSM Inter Working Unit) corresponds to an interface to various networks for data communications.
- *Operation and Support Subsystem - OSS*
- Operations and Support Subsystem (OSS) controls and monitors the GSM system.
- OSS is connected to the different components of the NSS, to BSC and also in charge of controlling the traffic load of the BSS.
- Equipment Identity Register (EIR) rests with OSS.
- EIR is a database that contains a list of all valid mobile equipment within the network, where each mobile station is identified by its International Mobile Equipment Identity (IMEI).
- EIR contains a list of IMEIs of all valid terminals.

- An IMEI is marked as invalid if it has been reported stolen or is not type approved.
- The EIR allows the MSC to forbid calls from this stolen or unauthorized terminals.
- Authentication Center (AUC) is responsible for the authentication of a subscriber.
- AUC is a protected database and stores a copy of the secret key stored in each subscriber's SIM card.

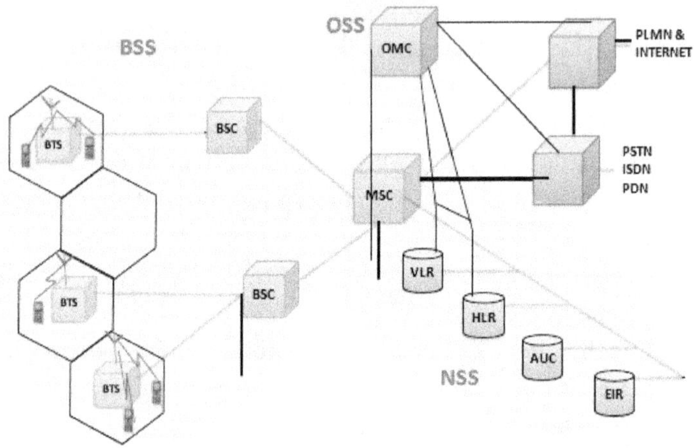

Figure 12: System Architecture of GSM

Handover procedure in GSM system OR What is handover / handoff ? How handoff is different from roaming?

- The process of handover or handoff within any cellular system is of great importance.

- It is a critical process and if performed incorrectly handover can result in the loss of the call.
- Dropped calls are particularly annoying to users and if the number of dropped calls rises, customer dissatisfaction increases and they are likely to change to another network.

Types of GSM handover

- Within the GSM system there are four types of handover that can be performed for GSM only systems:

  - **Intra-BTS handover:** This form of GSM handover occurs if it is required to change the frequency or slot being used by a mobile because of interference, or other reasons.
  - In this form of GSM handover, the mobile remains attached to the same base station transceiver, but change the channel or slot.
  - **Inter-BTS Intra BSC handover:** This GSM handover or GSM handoff occurs when the mobile is moved out of the coverage area of one BTS but into another controlled by the same BSC.
  - In this instance the BSC is able to perform the handover and it assigns a new channel and slot to the mobile, before releasing the old BTS from communicating with the mobile.
  - **Inter-BSC handover:** When the mobile is moved out of the range of cells controlled by one BSC, a more involved form of handover has to be performed, handing over not only from one BTS to another but one BSC to another.
  - For this the handover is controlled by the MSC.
  - **Inter-MSC handover:** This form of handover occurs when changing between networks. The two MSCs involved negotiate to control the handover.

GSM handover process

- Although there are several forms of GSM handover as detailed above, as far as the mobile is concerned, they are effectively seen as very similar. There are a number of stages involved in undertaking a GSM handover from one cell or base station to another.
- In GSM, which uses TDMA techniques the transmitter only transmits for one slot in eight, and similarly the receiver only receives for one slot in eight.
- As a result the RF section of the mobile could be idle for 6 slots out of the total eight.
- This is not the case because during the slots in which it is not communicating with the BTS, it scans the other radio channels looking for beacon frequencies that may be stronger or more suitable.
- In addition to this, when the mobile communicates with a particular BTS, one of the responses it makes is to send out a list of the radio channels of the beacon frequencies of neighboring BTSs via the Broadcast Channel (BCCH).
- The mobile scans these and reports back the quality of the link to the BTS. In this way the mobile assists in the handover decision and as a result this form of GSM handover is known as Mobile Assisted Hand over (MAHO).
- The network knows the quality of the link between the mobile and the BTS as well as the strength of local BTSs as reported back by the mobile.
- It also knows the availability of channels in the nearby cells. As a result it has all the information it needs to be able to make a decision about whether it needs to hand the mobile over from one BTS to another.
- If the network decides that it is necessary for the mobile to hand over, it assigns a new channel and time slot to the mobile. It informs the BTS and the mobile of the change.
- The mobile then retunes during the period it is not transmitting or receiving, i.e. in an idle period.

- A key element of the GSM handover is timing and synchronization. There are a number of possible scenarios that may occur dependent upon the level of synchronization.

Roaming

- In wireless telecommunications, roaming is a general term that refers to the extending of connectivity service in a location that is different from the home location where the service was registered. Roaming ensures that the wireless device keeps connected to the network, without losing the connection. The term "roaming" originates from the GSM (Global System for Mobile Communications) sphere; the term "roaming" can also be applied to the CDMA technology.

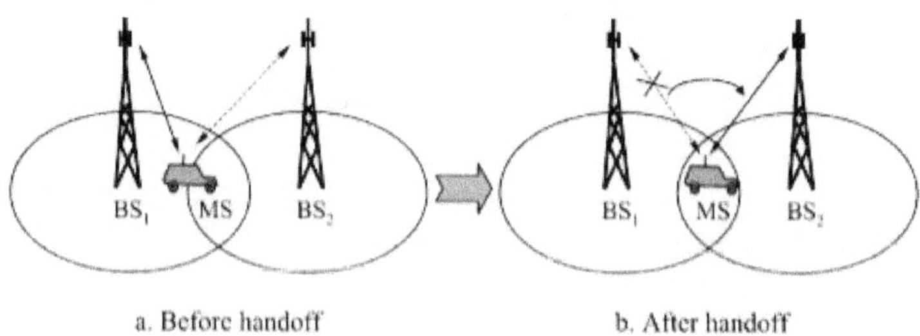

Figure 13: Handoff Process

Handoff

- In cellular telecommunications, the term handover or handoff refers to the process of transferring an ongoing call or data session from one channel connected to the core network to another.

- In satellite communications it is the process of transferring satellite control responsibility from one earth station to another without loss or interruption of service.

GSM Addresses and Identifiers

- **International Mobile Station Equipment Identity (IMEI):** It uniquely identifies a mobile station internationally. It is a kind of serial number.
- The IMEI is allocated by the equipment manufacturer and registered by the network operator, who stores it in the EIR.
- By means of IMEI one can recognize obsolete, stolen or non-functional equipment. The following are the parts of an IMEI:

  - Type Approval Code (TAC):- 6 decimal places, centrally assigned.
  - Final Assembly Code (FAC):- 6 decimal places, assigned by the manufacturer.
  - Serial Number (SNR):- 6 decimal places, assigned by the manufacturer.
  - Spare (SP):- 1 decimal place.

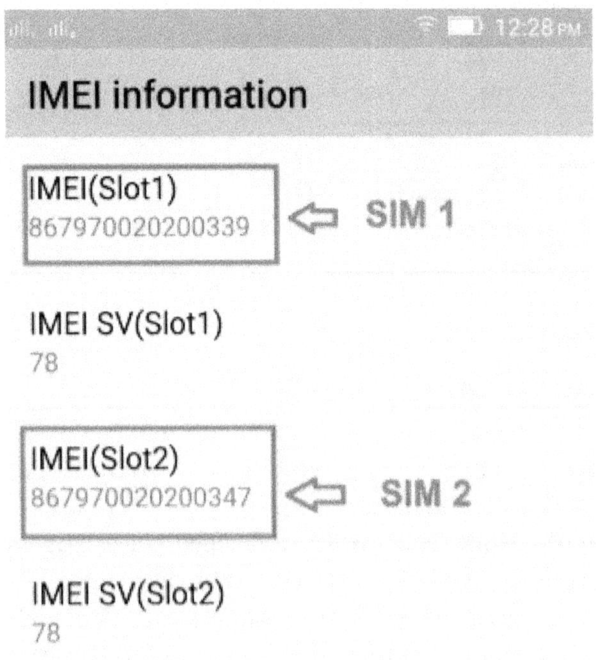

Figure 14: International Mobile Station Equipment Identity (IMEI)

- **International Mobile Subscriber Identity (IMSI):** Each registered user is uniquely identified by its international mobile subscriber identity (IMSI).
- It is stored in the subscriber identity module (SIM). A mobile station can only be operated if a SIM with valid IMSI is inserted into equipment with a valid IMEI.

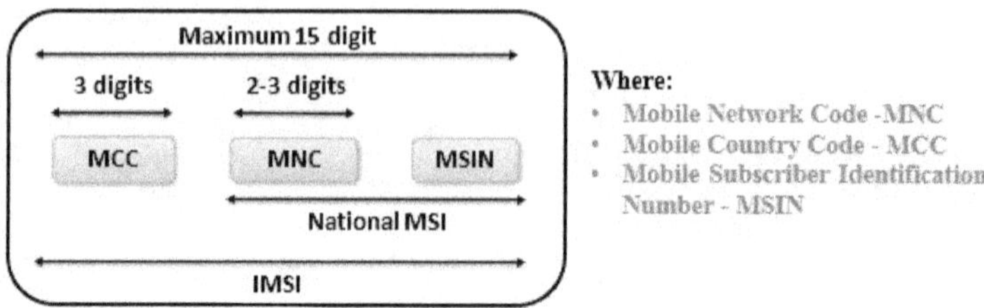

Figure 15: International Mobile Subscriber Identity (IMSI)

- The following are the parts of IMSI:-

  - Mobile Country Code (MCC):- 3 decimal places, internationally standardized.
  - Mobile Network Code (MNC):- 2 decimal places, for unique identification of mobile network within the country.
  - Mobile Subscriber Identification Number (MSIN):- Maximum 10 decimal places, identification number of the subscriber in the home mobile network.

- **Mobile Subscriber ISDN Number (MSISDN):** The real telephone number of a mobile station is the mobile subscriber ISDN number (MSISDN).
- It is assigned to the subscriber, such that a mobile station set can have several MSISDNs depending on the SIM.
- The MSISDN categories follow the international ISDN number plan and therefore have the following structure:-

  - Country Code (CC):- Up to 3 decimal places.
  - National Destination Code (NDC):- Typically 2-3 decimal places.
  - Subscriber Number (SN):- Maximum 10 decimal places.

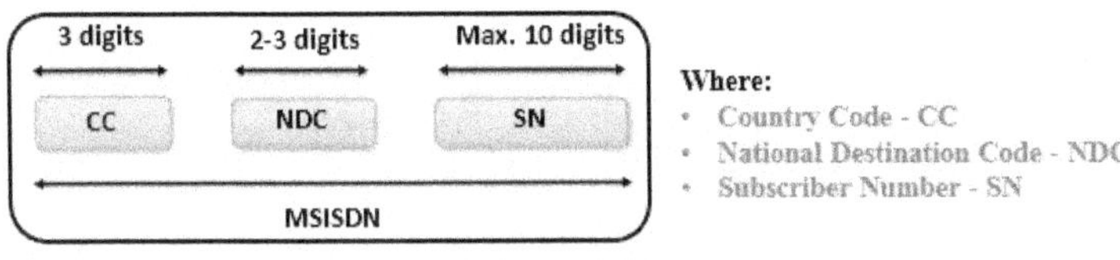

Figure 16: Mobile Subscriber ISDN Number (MSISDN)

- **Location Area Identity:** Each LA in a PLMN has own identifier called Location Area Identifier (LAI) which is structured hierarchically and unique. Example: 502-20-60001

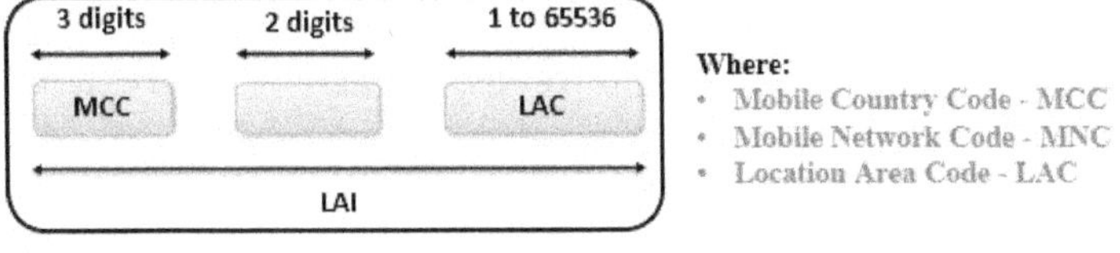

Figure 17: Location Area Identity:

- **Mobile Station Roaming Number (MSRN):** When a subscriber is roaming in another network, a temporary ISDN number assigned to the subscriber called MSRN.

  - MSRN assigned by the local VLR in charge of the mobile station and follows the structure of MSISDN.

- **Temporary Mobile Subscriber Identity (TMSI):** TMSI is a temporary identifier assigned by the serving VLR used in place of the IMSI for identification and addressing of the mobile station.

- ○ Together with the current location area, a TMSI allows a subscriber to identified uniquely.

- **Local Mobile Subscriber Identity (LMSI):** LMSI assigned by the VLR and stored in the HLR and used as a searching key for faster database access within the VLR.
- **Cell Identifier:** Within an LA, every cell has a unique Cell Identifier (CI) together with an LAI, a cell can be identified uniquely through Global Cell Identity (LAI & CI).

Call routing in GSM with block diagram

- Human interface is analog. However, the advancement in digital technology makes it very convenient to handle information in digital way.
- **Digitizer and source coding:** The user speech is digitized at 8 KHz sampling rate using Regular Pulse Excited–Linear Predictive Coder (RPE–LPC) with a Long Term Predictor loop where information from previous samples is used to predict the current sample.
- Each sample is then represented in signed 13-bit linear PCM value.
- This digitized data is passed to the coder with frames of 160 samples where encoder compresses these 160 samples into 260-bits GSM frames resulting in one second of speech compressed into 1625 bytes and achieving a rate of 13 Kbits/sec.
- **Channel coding:** This introduces redundancy into the data for error detection and possible error correction where the gross bit rate after channel coding is 22.8 kbps (or 456 bits every 20 ms).

- These 456 bits are divided into eight 57-bit blocks and the result is interleaved amongst eight successive time slot bursts for protection against burst transmission errors.
- **Interleaving:** This step rearranges a group of bits in a particular way to improve the performance of the error-correction mechanisms.
- The interleaving decreases the possibility of losing whole bursts during the transmission by dispersing the errors.

- **Ciphering:** This encrypts blocks of user data using a symmetric key shared by the mobile station and the BTS.
- **Burst formatting:** It adds some binary information to the ciphered block for use in synchronization and equalization of the received data.
- **Modulation:** The modulation technique chosen for the GSM system is the Gaussian Minimum Shift Keying (GMSK) where binary data is converted back into analog signal to fit the frequency and time requirements for the multiple access rules.
- This signal is then radiated as radio wave over the air.
- **Multipath and equalization:** An equalizer is in charge of extracting the 'right' signal from the received signal while estimating the channel impulse response of the GSM system and then it constructs an inverse filter.
- The received signal is then passed through the inverse filter.
- **Synchronization:** For successful operation of a mobile radio system, time and frequency synchronization are needed.
- Frequency synchronization is necessary so that the transmitter and receiver frequency match (in FDMA) while Time synchronization is necessary to identify the frame boundary and the bits within the frame (in TDMA).
- To avoid collisions of burst transmitted by MS with the adjacent timeslot such collisions, the Timing Advance technique is used where frame is advanced in time so that this offsets the delay due to greater distance.

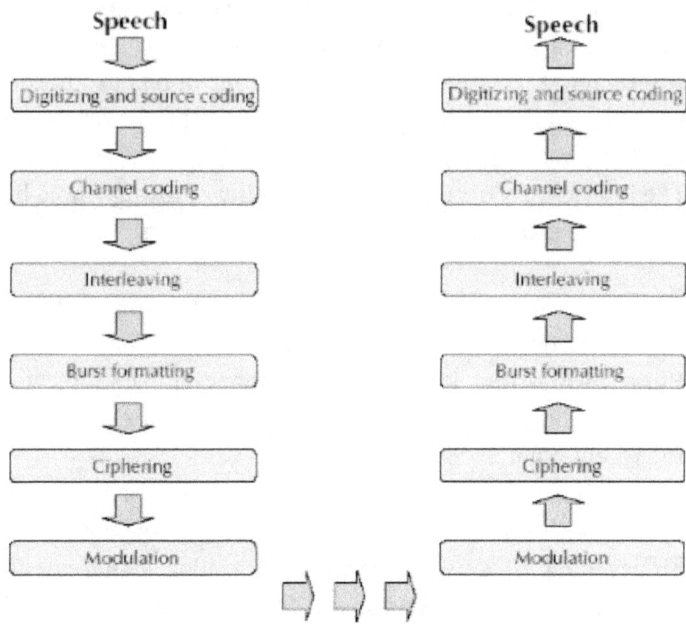

Figure 18: From speech to radio waves

- Using this technique and the triangulation of the intersection cell sites, the location of a mobile station can be determined from within the network.

Example

- The MSISDN number of a subscriber in Bangalore associated with Airtel network is

+919845XYYYYY which is a unique number and understood from anywhere in the world.

- Here, + means prefix for international dialing, 91 is the country code for India and 45 is the network operator's code (Airtel in this case).
- X is the level number managed by the network operator ranging from 0 to 9 while YYYYY is the subscriber code which, too, is managed by the operator.
- The call first goes to the local PSTN exchange where PSTN exchange looks at the routing table and determines that it is a call to a mobile network.
- PSTN forwards the call to the Gateway MSC (GMSC) of the mobile network.
- MSC enquires the HLR to determine the status of the subscriber. It will decide whether the call is to be routed or not. If MSC finds that the call can be processed, it will find out the address of the VLR where the mobile is expected to be present.
- **MSC/VLR**

  If VLR is that of a different PLMN, it will forward the call to the foreign PLMN through the Gateway MSC. If the VLR is in the home network, it will determine the Location Area (LA).

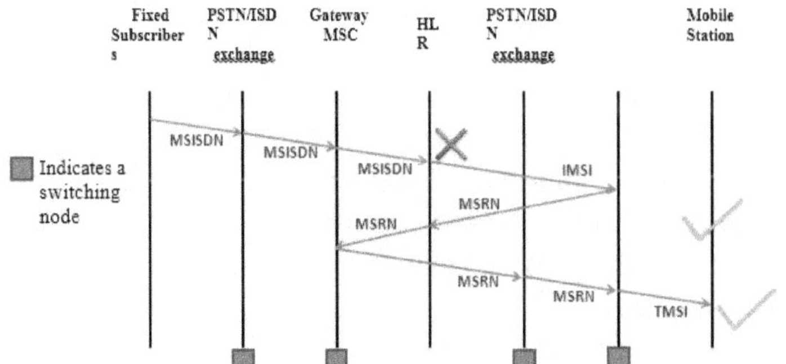

Figure 19: Call Routing for a mobile terminating call

- Within the LA, it will page and locate the phone and connect the call.

Signaling Protocol Structure in GSM

- Layer 1 is the physical layer which uses the channel structures over the air interface.
- Layer 2 is the data link layer and across the Um interface, the data link layer is a modified version of the LAPD protocol used in ISDN or X.25, called LAPDm.

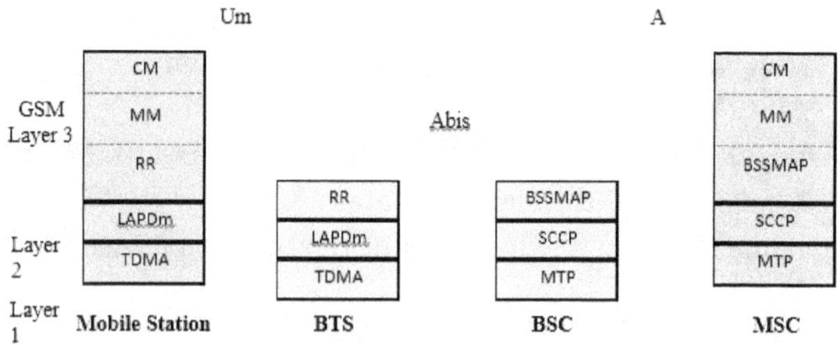

Figure 20: Signaling protocol structure in GSM

- Across the A interface, the Message Transfer Part layer 2 of Signaling System Number 7 is used.
- Layer 3 of the GSM signaling protocol is itself divided into three sub-layers:

  - **Radio Resources Management**: It controls the set-up, maintenance and termination of radio and fixed channels, including handovers.
  - **Mobility Management**: It manages the location updating and registration procedures as well as security and

authentication.

- **Connection Management:** It handles general call control and manages Supplementary Services and the Short Message Service.

Different GSM Services

- There are three types of services offered through GSM which are:
- Telephony (also referred as tele-services) Services
- *Teleservices or Telephony Services*
- A teleservices utilizes the capabilities of a Bearer Service to transport data, defining which capabilities are required and how they should setup.

  - **Voice Calls:** The most basic teleservices supported by GSM is telephony. This includes full rate speech at 13 Kbps and emergency calls, where the nearest emergency service provider is notified by dialing three digits.
  - **Videotext and Facsimile:** Another group of teleservices includes Videotext access, Teletext transmission, and Facsimile alternate speech and facsimile Group 3, automatic facsimile Group 3 etc.
  - **Short Text Messages:** SMS service is a text messaging which allow you to send and receive text messages on your GSM mobile phones.

- Data (also referred as bearer services) Services
- Supplementary Services

Bearer Services or Data Services

- Using your GSM phone to receive and send data is the essential building block leading to widespread mobile Internet access and mobile and mobile data transfer.
- GSM currently has a data transfer rate of 9.6k.
- New development that will push up data transfer rated for GSM users HSCSD are now available.

Supplementary Services

- Supplementary services are provided on top of teleservices or bearer services, and include features such as caller identification, call forwarding, call waiting, multi-party conversation. A brief description of supplementary services is given here:

  - **Multiparty Service or conferencing:** The multiparty service allows a mobile subscriber to establish multiparty conservations. That is, conservation between three or more subscribers to setup a conference calls. This service is only applicable to normal telephony.
  - **Call Waiting:** This service allows a mobile subscriber to be notified of an incoming call during a conversation. The subscriber can answer, reject or ignore the incoming call. Call waiting is applicable to all GSM telecommunications services using circuit switched connection.
  - **Call Hold:** This service allows a mobile subscriber to put an incoming call on hold and then resume this call. The call hold service is only applicable to normal telephony.
  - **Call Forwarding:** The call forwarding supplementary service is used to divert calls from the original recipient to another number, and is normally set up by the subscriber himself.
  - It can be used by the subscriber to divert calls from the Mobile Station when the subscriber is not available, and so to ensure that calls are not lost.

- ○ A typical scenario would be a salesperson turns off his mobile phone during a meeting with customer, but does not wish to lose potential sales leads while he is unavailable.
- ○ **Call Barring:** The concept of barring certain type of calls might seem to be a supplementary disservice rather than service.
- ○ However, there are times when the subscriber is not the actual user of the Mobile Station, and as a consequence may wish to limit its functionality, so as to limit charges incurred.
- ○ If the subscriber and users and one and same, the call barring may be useful to stop calls being routed to international destinations when they are route.
- ○ The reasons for this are because it is expected that are roaming subscriber will pay the charges incurred for international re-routing of calls.
- ○ So, GSM devised some flexible services that enable the subscriber to conditionally bar calls.

Introduction of GPRS

- GPRS is an abbreviation for General Packet Radio Service.
- GPRA is a means of providing packet switched data service with full mobility and wide area coverage on GSM networks.
- The GPRS service is designed to ultimately provide data transfer up to 14.4 kBps to 171.2 KBps.
- Deployment of GPRS networks allows a variety of new applications ranging from mobile e- commerce to mobile corporate VPN access.
- No dial-up modem connection is necessary.
- Offers fast connection set-up mechanism to offer a perception of being 'always on' or 'always connected'.
- Immediacy is one of the prime advantages of GPRS.

Basic Quality of Service in GPRS

- Allows definition of QoS profiles using the parameters of service precedence, reliability, delay and throughput.
- **Service precedence** is the priority of a service in relation to another service which can be high, normal or low.
- **Reliability** indicates the transmission characteristics required by an application and guarantees certain maximum values for the probability of loss, duplication, mis-sequencing and corruption of packets.
- **Delay** parameters define maximum values for the mean delay and the 95-percentile delay.
- **Throughput** specifies the maximum/peak bit rate and the mean bit rate.

GPRS functional architecture and its application

- GPRS uses the GSM architecture for voice.
- GPRS support nodes are responsible for the delivery and routing of data packets between the mobile stations and the external packet data networks (PDN).
- There are 2 types of support nodes which are given below:

Serving GPRS Support Node (SGSN)

- A SGSN is at the same hierarchical level as the MSC. Whatever functions MSC does for the voice, SGSN does the same for packet data.
- SGSN's tasks include packet switching, routing and transfer, mobility management, logical link management, and authentication and charging functions.
- SGSN processes registration of new mobile subscribers and keeps a record of their location inside a given service area.

- The location register of the SGSN stores location information and uses profiles of all GPRS users registered with the SGSN.
- SGSN sends queries to HLR to obtain profile data of GPRS subscribers. The SGSN is connected to the base station system with Frame Relay.

Gateway GPRS Support Node (GGSN)

- A GGSN acts as an interface between the GPRS backbone network and the external packet data network.
- GGSN's function is similar to that of a router in a LAN. GGSN maintains routing information that is necessary to tunnel the Protocol Data Units (PDUs) to the SGSNs that service particular mobile stations.
- It converts the GPRS packets coming from the SGSN into the appropriate packet data protocol (PDP) format for the data networks like internet or X.25, PDP sends these packets out on the corresponding packet data network.
- The readdressed packets are sent to the responsible SGSN. For this purpose, the GGSN stores the current SGSN address of the user and his or her profile in its location register.
- GGSN also performs authentication and charging functions related to data transfer.
- **SGSN**
  Some existing GSM network elements must be enhanced in order to support packet data. These are as following:

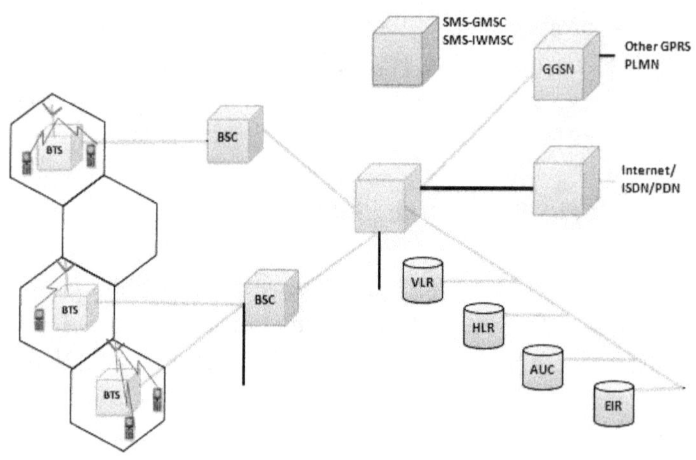

Figure 21: GPRS Architecture

Abbreviation:			
AUC	Authentication Center	MS	Mobile Station
BSC	Base Station Controller	MSC	Mobile Switching Center
BTS	Base Transceiver Station	PDN	Packet Data Network
EIR	Equipment Identity Register	PLMN	Public Land Mobile Network
GGSN	Gateway GPRS Support Node	SMSC	Short Message Service Center

Base Station System (BSS)

- BSS system needs enhancements to recognize and send packet data.
- This includes BTS upgrade to allow transportation of user data to the SGSN.
- Also, the BTS needs to be upgraded to support packet data transportation between the BTS and the MS (Mobile Station) over the radio.

Home Location Register (HLR)

- HLR needs enhancement to register GPRS user profiles and respond to queries originating from GSNs regarding these profiles.

Mobile Station (MS)

- The mobile station or the mobile phone for GPRS is different from that of GSM.

SMS Nodes

- SMS-GMSCs and SMS-IWMSCs are upgraded to support SMS transmission via the SGSN.0
- Optionally, the MSC/VLR can be enhanced for more efficient coordination of GPRS and non- GPRS services and functionality.
- GPRS uses two frequency bands at 45 MHz apart; viz., 890-915 MHz for uplink (MS to BTS), and 935-960 MHz for downlink (BTS to MS).

Applications of GPRS

- **Communications:** E-mail, fax, unified messaging and intranet/internet access, etc.
- **Value-added services:** Information services and games, etc.
- **E-commerce**: Retail, ticket purchasing, banking and financial trading, etc.
- **Location-based applications**: Navigation, traffic conditions, airline/rail schedules and location finder, etc.
- **Vertical applications**: Freight delivery, fleet management and sales-force automation.
- **Advertising:** It may be location sensitive. For example, a user entering a mall can receive advertisements specific to the stores in that mall.

Transmission Plane Protocol Architecture of GPRS

- Figure shows the protocol architecture of the GPRS transmission plane, providing transmission of user data and its associated signaling.
- The transmission plane consists of a layered protocol structure providing user data transfer, along with associated procedures that control the information transfer such as flow control, error detection, and error correction.
- Figure shows the layered protocol structure between the MS and the GGSN.

Air Interface

- The air interface is located between the MS and the BSS. The protocols used on the air interface are as follows:

  - **Radio link control/medium access control** (RLC/MAC): RLC provides a reliable radio link between the mobile and the BSS.
  - MAC controls the access signaling procedures to the GPRS radio channel, and the multiplexing of signaling and RLC blocks from different users onto the GSM physical channel.
  - **GSM-RF layer:** It is the radio subsystem that supports a certain number of logical channels.

o This layer is split into two sub layers: the radio frequency layer (RFL), which handles the radio and baseband part (physical channel management, modulation, demodulation, and transmission and reception of radio blocks), and the physical link layer (PLL), which manages control of the RFL (power control, synchronization, measurements, and channel coding/decoding).

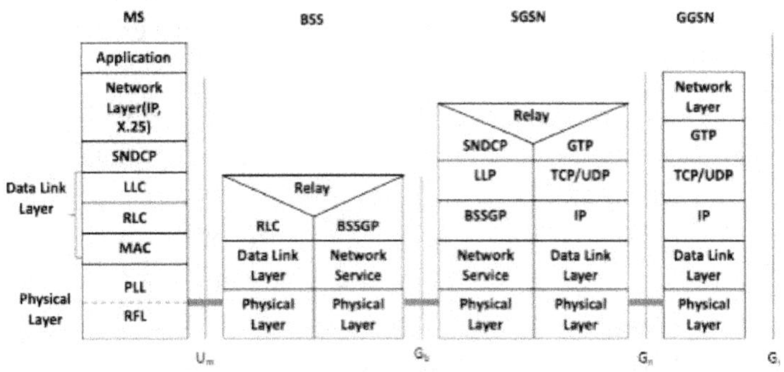

Figure 22: Transmission Plane and GPRS Protocol Stack

A relay function is implemented in the BSS to relay the LLC PDUs between the air interface and the Gb interface.

Gb Interface

- The Gb interface is located between the SGSN and the BSS. It supports data transfer in the transmission plane. The Gb interface supports the following protocols:

    ◦ **BSS GPRS protocol (BSSGP):** This layer conveys routing and QoS-related information between the BSS and SGSN.
    ◦ **Network service (NS):** It transports BSSGP PDUs and is based on a frame relay connection between the BSS and SGSN.
    ◦ A relay function is implemented in the BSS to relay the LLC PDUs between the air interface and the Gb interface.

        Gb Interface

    ◦ The Gb interface is located between the SGSN and the BSS. It supports data transfer in the transmission plane. The Gb interface supports the following protocols:

        ◦ **BSS GPRS protocol (BSSGP):** This layer conveys routing and QoS-related information between the BSS and SGSN.

- **Network service (NS):** It transports BSSGP PDUs and is based on a frame relay connection between the BSS and SGSN.
- A relay function is implemented in the SGSN to relay the packet data protocol (PDP) PDUs between the Gb and Gn interfaces.
- *Gn/Gp Interface*
- The Gn interface is located between two GSNs (SGSN or GGSN) within the same PLMN, while the Gp interface is between two GSNs in different PLMNs.
- The Gn/Gp interface is used for the transfer of packets between the SGSN and the GGSN in the transmission plane. The Gn/Gp interface supports the following protocols:

  - **GPRS tunneling protocol (GTP):** This protocol tunnels user data between the SGSN and GGSN in the GPRS backbone network. GTP operates on top of UDP over IP. The layers L1 and L2 of the Gn interfaces are not specified in the GSM/GPRS standard.
  - **User datagram protocol (UDP):** It carries GTP packet data units (PDUs) in the GPRS Core Network for protocols that do not need a reliable data link (e.g., IP).
  - **Internet protocol (IP):** This is the protocol used for routing user data and control signaling within the GPRS backbone network.

- *Interface between MS and SGSN*
- This interface supports the following protocols:

  - **Sub network-dependent convergence protocol (SNDCP):** This protocol maps the IP protocol to the underlying network. SNDCP also provides other functions such as compression, segmentation, and multiplexing of network layer messages.

- **Logical link control (LLC):** This layer provides a highly reliable logical link that is independent of the underlying radio interface protocols. LLC is also responsible for the GPRS ciphering.

-

PDP context activation procedure with respect to GPRS

- In GPRS network, MS registers itself with SGSN through a GPRS attach which establishes a logical link between the MS and the SGSN.
- To exchange data packets with external PDNs after a successful GPRS attach, an MS must apply for an address which is called **PDP (Packet Data Protocol) address**.
- For each session, a PDP context is created which contains PDP type (e.g. IPv4), PDP address assigned to the mobile station (e.g. 129.187.222.10), requested QoS and address of the GGSN that will function as an access point to the PDN.
- Such a context is stored in MS, SGSN and GGSN while with an active PDP context; the MS is 'visible' to the external PDN.
- A user may have several simultaneous PDP contexts active at a given time and user data is transferred transparently between MS and external data networks.
- Allocation of the PDP address can be static or dynamic.
- In case of static address, the network operator permanently assigns a PDP address to the user while in other case, a PDP address is assigned to the user upon the activation of a PDP context.
- Using the message **"activate PDP context request"**, MS informs the SGSN about the requested PDP context and if request is for dynamic PDP address assignment, the
- parameter PDP address will be left empty.

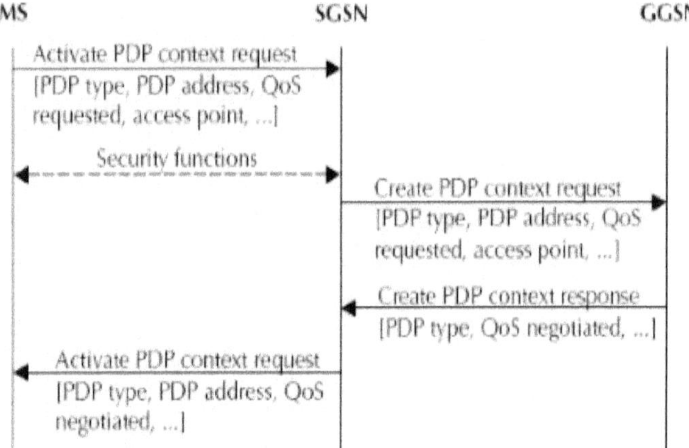

Figure 23: PDP Context Activation

- After necessary security steps, if authentication is successful, SGSN will send a 'create PDP context request' message to the GGSN, the result of which is a confirmation message 'create PDP context response' from the GGSN to the SGSN, which contains the PDP address.
- SGSN updates its PDP context table and confirms the activation of the new PDP context to the MS.
-

How the packets are routed in GPRS. Explain GPRS packet routing for Inter & Intra PLMN.

- Routing is the process of how packets are routed in GPRS.
- Here, the example assumes two intra-PLMN backbone networks of different PLMNs. Intra- PLMN backbone networks connect GSNs of the same PLMN or the same network operator.
- These intra-PLMN networks are connected with an inter-PLMN backbone while an inter-PLMN backbone network connects GSNs of different PLMNs and operators. However, a

roaming agreement is necessary between two GPRS network providers.

○

○ Disconnection from the GPRS network is called GPRS detach in which all the resources are released.

○ Gateways between PLMNs and external inter-PLMN backbone are called border gateways which perform security functions to protect the private intra-PLMN backbones against malicious attacks.

○ Let's say that GPRS MS located in PLMN1 sends IP packets to a host connected to the IP network (e.g. to a Web server connected to the Internet).

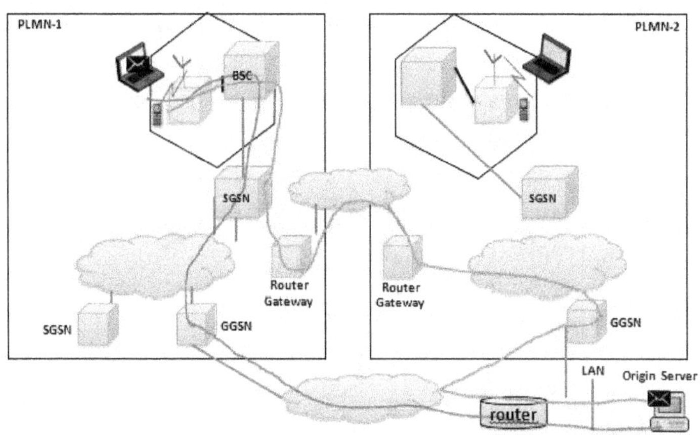

Figure 24: GPRA Packet Routing

•

• SGSN that the MS is registered with encapsulates the IP packets coming from the mobile station, examines the PDP context and routes them through the intra-PLMN GPRS backbone to the appropriate GGSN.

• GGSN de-encapsulates the packets and sends them out on the IP network, where IP routing mechanisms are used to transfer the packets to the access router of the destination network and finally, delivers the IP packets to the host.

- Let us also say that home-PLMN of the mobile station is PLMN2.
- An IP address has been assigned to MS by the GGSN of PLMN2 and so, MS's IP address has the same network prefix as the IP address of the GGSN in PLMN2.
- Correspondent host is now sending IP packets to the MS onto the IP network and are routed to the GGSN of PLMN2 (the home-GGSN of the MS). The latter queries the HLR and obtains the information that the MS is currently located in PLMN1.
- It encapsulates the incoming IP packets and tunnels them through the inter-PLMN GPRS backbone to the appropriate SGSN in PLMN1 while the SGSN de-encapsulates the packets and delivers them to the MS.
- HLR stores the user profile, the current SGSN address and the PDP addresses for every GPRS user in the PLMN.
- When the MS registers with a new SGSN, HLR will send the user profile to the new SGSN.
- Signaling path between GGSN and HLR may be used by the GGSN to query a user's location and profile in order to update its location register.
-

Data services in GPRS

- Any user is likely to use either of the two modes of the GPRS network:

  - Application mode
  - Tunneling mode

- In **application mode**, user uses the GPRS mobile phone to access the applications running on the phone itself. The phone here acts as the end user device.
- In **tunneling mode**, user uses GPRS interface as an access to the network as the end user device would be a large footprint device

like laptop computer or a small footprint device like PDA.
- The mobile phone will be connected to the device and used as a modem to access the wireless data network.
·

Billing and Charging in GPRS

- For voice networks tariffs are generally based on distance and time means that user pay more for long distance calls.
- On other hand, in data services, minimum charging information that must be collected are:

  - Destination and source addresses
  - Usage of radio interface
  - Usage of external Packet Data Networks
  - Usage of the packet data protocol addresses
  - Usage of general GPRS resources and location of the Mobile Station

- A GPRS network needs to be able to count packets to charging customers for the volume of packets they send and receive.
- Various business models exist for charging customers as billing of services can be based on the transmitted data volume, the type of service, the chosen QoS profile, etc.
- GPRS call records are generated in the GPRS Service Nodes.
- Packet counts are passed to a Charging Gateway that generates Call Detail Records that are sent to the billing system.
·

Limitations of GPRS

- A GPRS is a new enabling mobile data service which offers a major improvement in spectrum efficiency, capability and functionality compared with today's non-voice mobile services.
- However, it is important to note that there are some limitations with GPRS, which can be summarized as:
- *Limited Cell Capacity for All Users*

- GPRS does impact a network's existing cell capacity.
- There are only limited radio resources that can be deployed for different uses - use for one purpose precludes simultaneous use for another.
- For example, voice and GPRS calls both use the same network resources. If tariffing and billing are not done properly, this may have impact on revenue.
- *Speeds Much Lower in Reality*
- Achieving the theoretical maximum GPRS data transmission speed of 172.2 kbps would require a single user taking over all eight timeslots without any error protection.
- Clearly, it is unlikely that a network operator will allow all timeslots to be used by a single GPRS user.
- Additionally, the initial GPRS terminals are expected be severely limited - supporting only one, two or three timeslots.
- The bandwidth available to a GPRS user will therefore be severely limited.
- The reality is that mobile networks are always likely to have lower data transmission speeds than fixed networks.
- *Transit Delays*
- GPRS packets are sent in all different directions to reach the same destination.
- This opens up the potential for one or some of those packets to be lost or corrupted during the data transmission over the radio link.
- The GPRS standards recognize this inherent feature of wireless packet technologies and incorporate data integrity and retransmission strategies.
- However, the result is that potential transit delays can occur.
-

Mobile IP

- The term "Mobile" in Mobile IP signifies that, while a user is connected to applications across the Internet and the user's point of attachment changes dynamically, all connections are maintained despite the change in underlying network properties.

- Similar to the handoff/roaming situation in a cellular network.
- Mobile IP allows the mobile node to use two IP addresses called home address and care of address.
- The home address is static and known to everybody as the identity of the host.
- The care of address changes at each new point of attachment and can be thought of as the mobile node's location specific address.

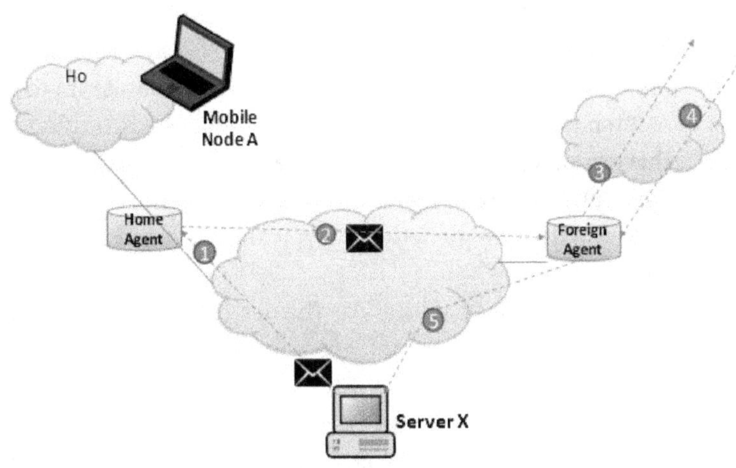

Figure 25: Mobile IP

- Let's take the case of mobile node (A) and another host (server X). The following steps take place:
- Server X wants to transmit an IP datagram to node A.
- The home address of A is advertised and known to X.
- X does not know whether A is in the home network or somewhere else.
- Therefore, X sends the packet to A with A's home address as the destination IP address in the IP header.
- The IP datagram is routed to A's home network.

- At the A's home network, the incoming IP datagram is intercepted by the home agent.
- The home agent discovers that A is in a foreign network.
- A care of address has been allocated to A by this foreign network and available with the home agent.
- The home agent encapsulates the entire datagram inside a new IP datagram, with A's care of address in the IP header.
- This new datagram with the care of address as the destination address is retransmitted by the home agent.
- At the foreign network, the incoming IP datagram is intercepted by the foreign agent. The foreign agent is the counterpart of the home agent in the foreign network. The foreign agent strips off the outer IP header, and delivers the original datagram to A.
- A intends to respond to this message and sends traffic to X. In this example, X is not mobile; therefore X has a fixed IP address.
- For routing A's IP datagram to X, each datagram is sent to some router in the foreign network. Typically, this router is the foreign agent.
- A uses X's IP static address as the destination address in the IP header.
- The IP datagram from A to X travels directly across the network, using X's IP address as the destination address.
- Discovery - A mobile node uses a discovery procedure to identify prospective home agents and foreign agents.
- Registration - A mobile node uses a registration procedure to inform its home agent of its care- of address.
- Tunneling - Tunneling procedure is used to forward IP datagrams from a home address to a care of address.
-

Wireless Application Protocol

- WAP is an application communication protocol.
- It is designed for access to Internet and advanced telephony services from mobile phones.
- WAP uses mark-up language – WML.

- WAP can be used from variety of 2G and 3G networks.
- GPRS and 3G are more suited for these applications.
-

WAP Protocol Stack

- Wireless Application Environment - WAE

  - User agent which is the browser or a client program.
  - Wireless Markup Language (WML) which is a lightweight markup language optimized for use in wireless devices.

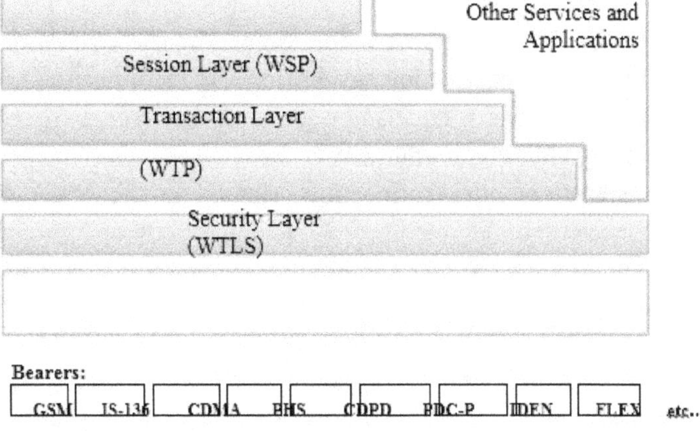

-

  - WML Script which is a lightweight client side scripting language.

- Wireless Telephony Application(WTP):

  - WAP Push Architecture which allow for mechanisms to allow origin servers to deliver content to the terminal without the terminal requesting for it.

- ○ Primary objective of WAE is to provide an interoperable environment to build services in wireless space.
- ○ Content is transported using standard protocols in the WWW domain and an optimized HTTP like protocol in the wireless domain.
- ○ WAE architecture allows all content and services to be hosted on standard Web Servers when all content is located using WWW standard URLs.
- ○ WAE enhances some of the WWW standards to reflect some of the telephony network characteristics.

- Wireless Session Protocol(WSP):

  - ○ Unlike HTTP, WSP has been designed by the WAP Forum to provide fast connection suspension and reconnection.
  - ○ WSP provides a consistent interface between two session services like client and server.
  - ○ WSP offers both connection-oriented and connectionless service.

- Wireless Transaction Protocol(WTP):

  - ○ It runs on top of a datagram service such as User Datagram Protocol (UDP) and is part of the standard suite of TCP/IP protocols used to provide a simplified protocol suitable for low bandwidth wireless stations.
  - ○ WTP supports class of transaction service, optional user-to-user reliability, PDU concatenation and asynchronous transaction.

- Wireless Transport Layer Security(WTLS):

  - ○ WTLS incorporates security features that are based upon the established Transport Layer Security(TLS) protocol standard.

- It provides data integrity, privacy, authentication, denial of service protection.

- Wireless Datagram Protocol(WDP):

  - WDP is transport layer protocol in WAP architecture.
  - WDP operates above data capable bearer services supported by various network type general transport service.
  - It allows WAP to be bearer-independent by adapting the transport layer of the underlying bearer.
  - The WDP presents a consistent data format to the higher layers of the WAP protocol stack.

-

Cordless System

- Cordless system is a general term of cordless telephones and cordless telecommunication systems.
- Cord means a wire, so, a cordless system means wireless system.
- A cordless telephone is known as a portable telephone and it acts as a standard phone.
- A base station communicates with the cordless handset through radio waves, and this usually only works within a limited range
- like residence or office.

Figure 26: Cordless Phone

- Example: Digital Enhanced Cordless Telecommunications (DECT) Phone.

Wireless Local Loop - WLL

- WLL is a system that connects subscribers to the local telephone station wirelessly.
- In telephone, a loop is circuit line from subscriber's phone to line-terminating equipment at the central office.
- Implementation of a local loop especially in rural areas used to remain a risk for many operators due to fewer users and increased cost of materials.
- So, Wireless local loop (WLL) has introduced which solves most of these problems.
- It is also known as fixed wireless systems.

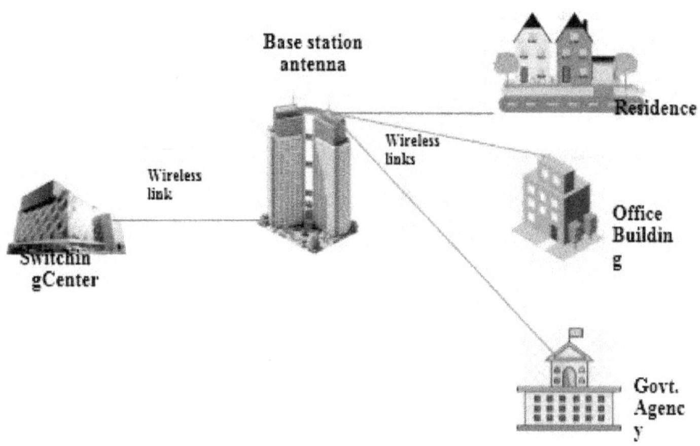

Figure 27: Configuration of WLL

Wireless Broadband

- It is known as Wireless Metropolitan Area Network (Wireless MAN) / Wireless Interoperability Microwave Access (WiMAX).
- IEEE 802.16 standard released in April 2002.
- It offers an alternative to high bandwidth wired access networks like fiber optic, cable modems and DSL.
- It provides network access to buildings through exterior antennas communicating with radio base stations.
- Networks can be created in just weeks by deploying a small number of base stations on buildings or poles to create high capacity wireless access systems.

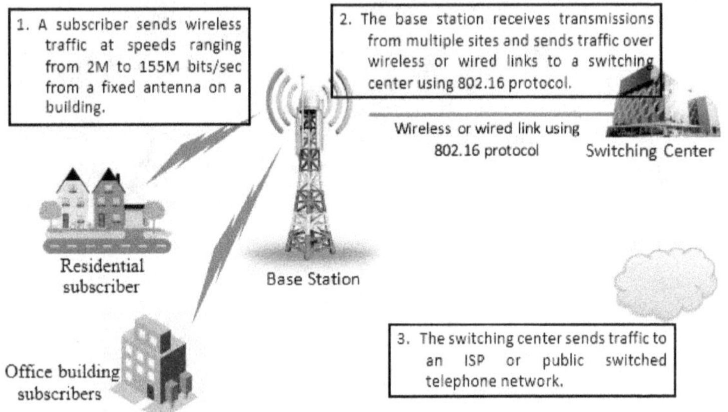

Figure 28: Deployment of WiMax – IEEE 802.16

Sub-standards of IEEE 802.16

- IEEE 802.16.1 - Air interface for 10 to 66 GHz
- IEEE 802.16.2 - Coexistence of broadband wireless access systems
- IEEE 802.16.3 - Air interface for licensed frequencies, 2 to 11 GHz

4

Wireless LAN

Introduction of Wireless LAN

- It is a network that allows devices to connect and communicate wirelessly.
- Unlike a traditional wired LAN, in which devices communicate over Ethernet cables, devices on a WLAN communicate via Wi-Fi.
- Mobile users can access information and network resources through wireless LAN as they attend meetings, collaborate with other users, or move to other locations in the premises.
- WLAN is not a replacement for the wired infrastructure. It implemented as an extension to a wired LAN within a building or campus. Wireless LAN is commercially known as WIFI or Wi-Fi.
- Wi-Fi is an acronym for Wireless Fidelity.
- In the corporate enterprise, wireless LANs are usually implemented as the final link between the existing wired network and a group of client computers, giving these users wireless access to the full resources and services of the corporate network across a building or campus setting.

Wireless LAN advantages:

- **Availability of low-cost portable equipment:** Due to the technology enhancements, the equipment cost that are required for WLAN set-up have reduced a lot.
- **Mobility**: An increasing number of LAN users are becoming mobile. These mobile users require that they are connected to the network regardless of where they are because they want simultaneous access to the network.
- This makes the use of cables, or wired LANs, impractical if not impossible. Wireless LAN can provide users mobility, which is likely to increase productivity, user convenience and various service opportunities.
- **Installation speed and simplicity:** Wireless LANs are very easy to install. There is no requirement for wiring every workstation and every room.
- This ease of installation makes wireless LANs inherently flexible. If a workstation must be moved, it can be done easily and without additional wiring, cable drops or reconfiguration of the network.
- **Installation flexibility:** If a company moves to a new location, the wireless system is much easier to move than ripping up all of the cables that a wired system would have snaked throughout the building.
- This also provides portability. Wireless technology allows network to go anywhere wire cannot reach.
- **Reduced cost of ownership:** While the initial cost of wireless LAN can be higher than the cost of wired LAN hardware, it is envisaged that the overall installation expenses and life cycle costs can be significantly lower.
- Long-term cost-benefits are greater in dynamic environment requiring frequent moves and changes.
- **Scalability:** Wireless LAN can be configured in a variety of topologies to meet the users need and can be easily scaled to cover a large area with thousands of users roaming within it.

Wireless LAN disadvantages

- Lower reliability due to susceptibility of radio transmission to noise and interference.
- Fluctuation of the strength of the received signal through multiple paths causing fading.
- Vulnerable to eavesdropping leading to security problem.
- Limited data rate because of the use of spread spectrum transmission techniques enforced to ISM band users.

Types of wireless LAN

- Types of Wireless LAN are: 1. 802.11

1. HyperLAN
2. HomeRF
3. Bluetooth
4. MANET

Ad hoc verses infrastructure mode

- In Ad hoc mode, there is no access point or infrastructure.
- A number of mobile stations from a cluster communicate with each other.
- Only require 802.11 client radios in the client devices that connect to the network.
- Because there is no access point or WLAN controller and the stations are within range of each other, data transmitted by a particular source station travels directly to the applicable destination station.

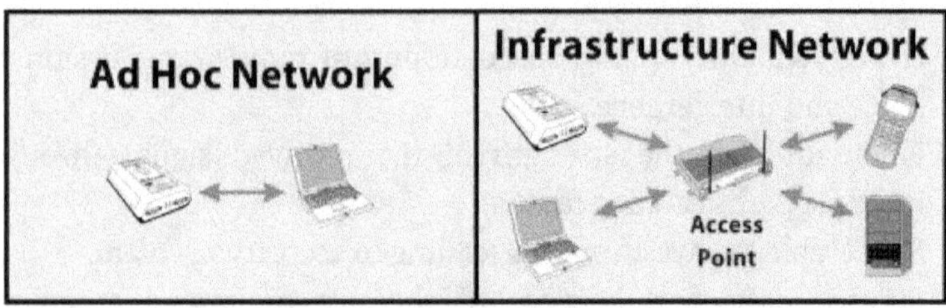

Figure 1: Ad hoc Vs Infrastructure Mode

- In infrastructure mode, the mobile station-MS are connected to a abase station or access point.
- This is similar to a star network where all the mobile stations are attached to the base station.
- Through a protocol the base station manages the dialogue between the AP and MS.
- Most companies, public hotspots, and homeowners implement infrastructure WLANs. In this configuration, one or more access points interface wireless mobile devices to the distribution system.
- Each access point forms a radio cell, also called a basic service set (BSS), which enables wireless users located within the cell to connect to the access point.
- This allows users to communicate with other wireless users, as well as with servers and network applications connecting to the distribution system.
- A company, for example, can use this configuration to enable employees to access corporate applications and the Internet from anywhere within the facility.
-

IEEE 802 Architecture

- This architecture was developed by the IEEE 802 committee and has been adopted by all organizations working on the specification of LAN standards. It is generally referred to as the IEEE 802 reference model.
- Working from the bottom up, the lowest layer of the IEEE 802 reference model corresponds to the physical layer of the OSI model and includes such functions as:

  - Encoding/decoding of signals (e.g., PSK, QAM, etc.)
  - Preamble generation/removal (for synchronization)
  - Bit transmission/reception

- For some of the IEEE 802 standards, the physical layer is further subdivided into sub layers.
- In the case of IEEE 802.11, two sub layers are defined:

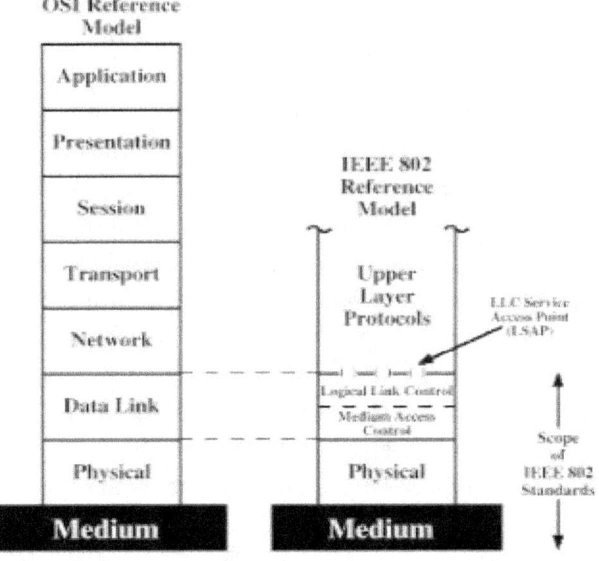

Figure 2: IEEE 802 Protocol Layers Compared to OSI Model

- **Physical layer convergence procedure (PLCP)**: Defines a method of mapping 802.11 MAC layer protocol data units (MPDUs) into a framing format suitable for sending and receiving user data and management information between two or more stations using the associated PMD sub layer.
- **Physical medium dependent sub layer (PMD)**: Defines the characteristics of, and method of transmitting and receiving, user data through a wireless medium between two or more stations
- Above the physical layer are the functions associated with providing service to LAN users. These include

- ○ On transmission, assemble data into a frame with address and error detection fields.
- ○ On reception, disassemble frame, and perform address recognition and error detection.
- ○ Govern access to the LAN transmission medium.
- ○ Provide an interface to higher layers and perform flow and error control.

- These are functions typically associated with OSI layer 2. The set of functions the last bullet item is grouped into a logical link control (LLC) layer. The functions in the first three bullet items are treated as a separate layer, called medium access control (MAC).
- The separation is done for the following reasons:

  - ○ The logic required to manage access to a shared-access medium is not found in traditional layer 2 data link control.
  - ○ For the same LLC, several MAC options may be provided.

IEEE 802.11 architecture and services

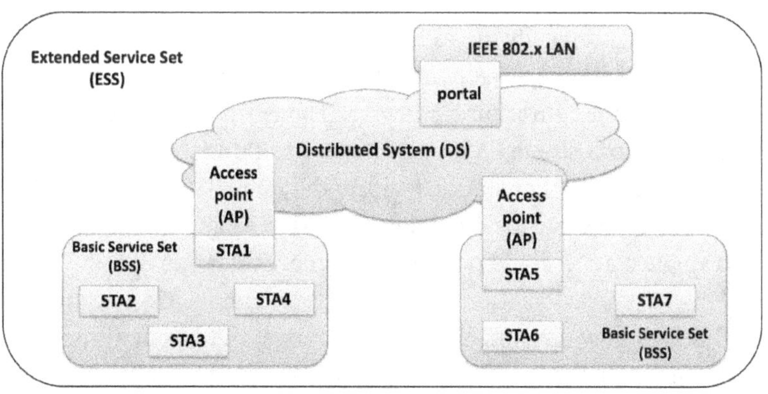

Figure 3: IEEE 802.11 Architecture

- The smallest building block of a wireless LAN is a basic service set (BSS), which consists of some number of stations executing the same MAC protocol and competing for access to the same shared wireless medium.
- A BSS may be isolated or it may connect to a backbone distribution system (DS) through an access point (AP).
- The AP functions as a bridge and a relay point. In a BSS, client stations do not communicate directly with one another.
- Rather, if one station in the BSS wants to communicate with another station in the same BSS, the MAC frame is first sent from the originating station to the AP, and then from the AP to the destination station.
- Similarly, a MAC frame from a station in the BSS to a remote station is sent from the local station to the AP and then relayed by the AP over the DS on its way to the destination station.
- The BSS generally corresponds to what is referred to as a cell in the literature. The DS can be a switch, a wired network, or a wireless network.
- When all the stations in the BSS are mobile stations, with no connection to other BSSs, the BSS is called an independent BSS (IBSS).
- An IBSS is typically an ad hoc network. In an IBSS, the stations all communicate directly, and no AP is involved.
- A simple configuration is shown in Figure, in which each station belongs to a single BSS; that is, each station is within wireless range only of other stations within the same BSS.
- It is also possible for two BSSs to overlap geographically, so that a single station could participate in more than one BSS.
- Further, the association between a station and a BSS is dynamic. Stations may turn off, come within range, and go out of range.
- An extended service set (ESS) consists of two or more basic service sets interconnected by a distribution system.

- Typically, the distribution system is a wired backbone LAN but can be any communications network.
- The extended service set appears as a single logical LAN to the logical link control (LLC) level.
- Figure indicates that an access point (AP) is implemented as part of a station; the AP is the logic within a station that provides access to the DS by providing DS services in addition to acting as a station.
- To integrate the IEEE 802.11 architecture with a traditional wired LAN, a portal is used. The portal logic is implemented in a device, such as a bridge or router, that is part of the wired LAN and that is attached to the DS.
- *IEEE 802.11 Services*
- IEEE 802.11 defines nine services that need to be provided by the wireless LAN to provide functionality equivalent to that which is inherent to wired LANs.
- It is categories with two ways of categorizing them.

  1. The service provider can be either the station or the distribution system (DS).

     ◦ Station services are implemented in every 802.11 station, including access point (AP) stations.
     ◦ Distribution services are provided between basic services sets (BSSs); these services may be implemented in an AP or in another special purpose device attached to the distribution system.

  1. Three of the services are used to control IEEE 802.11 LAN access and confidentiality.

     ◦ Six of the services are used to support delivery of MAC service data units (MSDUs) between stations.
     ◦ The MSDU is the block of data passed down from the MAC user to the MAC layer; typically this is a LLC PDU If the MSDU

is too large to be transmitted in a single MAC frame, it may be fragmented and transmitted in a series of MAC frames.

- **Distribution of Messages within a DS**: The two services involved with the distribution of messages within a DS are distribution and integration.
- Distribution is the primary service used by stations to exchange MAC frames when the frame must traverse the DS to get from a station in one BSS to a station in another BSS.
- For example, suppose a frame is to be sent from station 2 (STA 2) to STA 7 in Figure.
- The frame is sent from STA 2 to STA 1, which is the AP for this BSS. The AP gives the frame to the DS, which has the job of directing the frame to the AP associated with STA 5 in the target BSS.
- STA 5 receives the frame and forwards it to STA 7. How the message is transported through the DS is beyond the scope of the IEEE 802.11 standard.
- If the two stations that are communicating are within the same BSS, then the distribution service logically goes through the single AP of that BSS.
- The integration service enables transfer of data between a station on an IEEE 802.11 LAN and a station on an integrated IEEE 802.x LAN.
- The term integrated refers to a wired LAN that is physically connected to the DS and whose stations may be logically connected to an IEEE 802.11 LAN via the integration service.
- The integration service takes care of any address translation and media conversion logic required for the exchange of data.

Service	Provider	Used to support
Association	Distribution System	MSDU delivery
Authentication	Station/AP	LAN access and security
Deauthentication	Station/AP	LAN access and security
Disassociation	Distribution System	MSDU delivery
Distribution	Distribution System	MSDU delivery
Integration	Distribution System	MSDU delivery
MSDU delivery	Station/AP	MSDU delivery
Privacy	Station/AP	LAN access and security
Reassociation	Distribution System	MSDU delivery

MSDU – MAC Service Data Unit

Figure 4: IEEE 802.11 Services

Association Related Services:

- The primary purpose of the MAC layer is to transfer MSDUs between MAC entities; this purpose is fulfilled by the distribution service.
- For that service to function, it requires information about stations within the ESS, which is provided by the association-related services.
- Before the distribution service can deliver data to or accept data from a station, that station must be associated. Before looking at the concept of association, we need to describe the concept of mobility.
- The standard defines three transition types based on mobility:

- **No transition:** A station of this type is either stationary or moves only within the direct communication range of the communicating stations of a single BSS.
- **BSS transition:** This is defined as a station movement from one BSS to another BSS within the same ESS. In this case, delivery of data to the station requires that the addressing capability be able to recognize the new location of the station.
- **ESS transition:** This is defined as a station movement from a BSS in one ESS to a BSS within another ESS.
- This case is supported only in the sense that the station can move. Maintenance of upper-layer connections supported by 802.11 cannot be guaranteed. In fact, disruption of service is likely to occur.

- To deliver a message within a DS, the distribution service needs to know where the destination station is located.
- Specifically, the DS needs to know the identity of the AP to which the message should be delivered in order for that message to reach the destination station.
- To meet this requirement, a station must maintain an association with the AP within its current BSS. Three services relate to this requirement:

- **Association:** Establishes an initial association between a station and an AP Before a station can transmit or receive frames on a wireless LAN, its identity and address must be known.
- For this purpose, a station must establish an association with an AP within a particular BSS. The AP can then communicate this information to other APs within the ESS to facilitate routing and delivery of addressed frames.
- **Reassociation:** Enables an established association to be transferred from one AP to another, allowing a mobile station to move from one BSS to another.

- ○ **Disassociation**: A notification from either a station or an AP that an existing association is terminated.
- ○ A station should give this notification before leaving an ESS or shutting down. However, the MAC management facility protects itself against stations that disappear without notification.

- *Access and Privacy Services:*
- There are two characteristics of a wired LAN that are not inherent in a wireless LAN.
- In order to transmit over a wired LAN, a station must be physically connected to the LAN. On the other hand, with a wireless LAN, any station within radio range of the other devices on the LAN can transmit. In a sense, there is a form of authentication with a wired LAN, in that it requires some positive and presumably observable action to connect a station to a wired LAN.
- Similarly, in order to receive a· transmission from a station that is part of a wired LAN, the receiving station must also be attached to the wired LAN. On the other hand, with a wireless LAN, any station within radio range can receive. Thus, a wired LAN provides a degree of privacy, limiting reception of data to stations connected to the LAN.
- IEEE 802.11 defines three services that provide a wireless LAN with these two features:
- Authentication:
- Used to establish the identity of stations to each other. In a wired LAN, it is generally assumed that access to a physical connection conveys authority to connect to the LAN.
- This is not a valid assumption for a wireless LAN, in which connectivity is achieved simply by having an attached antenna that is properly tuned.
- The authentication service is used by stations to establish their identity with stations they wish to communicate with IEEE 802.11 supports several authentication schemes and allows for

expansion of the functionality of these schemes.

- The standard does not mandate any particular authentication scheme, which could range from relatively unsecure
- handshaking to public key encryption schemes.
- However, IEEE 802.11 requires mutually acceptable, successful authentication before a station can establish an association with an AP.
- De-authentication:
- This service is invoked whenever an existing authentication is to be terminated.
- Privacy:
- Used to prevent the contents of messages from being read by other than the intended recipient. The standard provides for the optional use of encryption to assure privacy.
-

IEEE 802.11 Medium access control

- The IEEE 802.11 MAC layer covers three functional areas: reliable data delivery, medium access control, and security.
- *Reliable Data Delivery*
- As with any wireless network, a wireless LAN using the IEEE 802.11 physical and MAC layers is subject to considerable unreliability.
- Noise, interference, and other propagation effects result in the loss of a significant number of frames.
- Even with error-correction codes, a number of MAC frames may not successfully be received.
- This situation can be dealt with by reliability mechanisms at a higher layer, such as TCP.
- However, timers used for retransmission at higher layers are typically on the order of seconds.
- It is therefore more efficient to deal with errors at the MAC level. For this purpose, IEEE 802.11 includes a frame exchange protocol.

- When a station receives a data frame from another station, it returns an acknowledgment (ACK) frame to the source station.
- This exchange is treated as an atomic unit, not to be interrupted by a transmission from any other station.
- If the source does not receive an ACK within a short period of time, either because its data frame was damaged or because the returning ACK was damaged, the source retransmits the frame.
- Thus, the basic data transfer mechanism in IEEE 802.11 involves an exchange of two frames.
- To further enhance reliability, a four-frame exchange may be used. In this scheme, a source first issues a request to send (RTS) frame to the destination.
- The destination then responds with a clear to send (CTS). After receiving the CTS, the source transmits the data frame, and the destination responds with an ACK.
- The RTS alerts all stations that are within reception range of the source that an exchange is under way; these stations refrain from transmission in order to avoid a collision between two
- frames transmitted at the same time.
- Similarly, the CTS alert all stations that are within reception range of the destination that an exchange is under way.
- The RTS/CTS portion of the exchange is a required function of the MAC but may be disabled.
- *Medium Access Control*
- The 802.11 working group considered two types of proposals for a MAC algorithm: **distributed access protocols**, which, like Ethernet, distribute the decision to transmit over all the nodes using a carrier-sense mechanism.
- **Centralized access protocols**, which involve regulation of transmission by a centralized decision maker.
- A distributed access protocol makes sense for an ad hoc network of peer workstations (typically an IBSS) and may also be attractive in other wireless LAN configurations that consist primarily of busty traffic.

- A centralized access protocol is natural for configurations in which a number of wireless stations are interconnected with each other and some sort of base station that attaches to a backbone wired LAN; it is especially useful if some of the data is time sensitive or high priority.

-

IEEE 802.11 physical layer

- The physical layer for IEEE 802.11 has been issued in four stages.
- The first part, simply called IEEE 802.11, includes the MAC layer and three physical layer specifications, two in the 2.4-GHz band (ISM) and one in the infrared, all operating at 1 and 2 Mbps. IEEE 802.11a operates in the 5-GHz band at data rates up to 54 Mbps.
- IEEE 802.11b operates in the 2.4-GHz band at 5.5 and 11 Mbps.
- IEEE 802.11g also operates in the 2.4-GHz band, at data rates up to 54 Mbps.
- Figure shows the relationship among the various standards developed for the physical layer, and table provides details.
- **Direct sequence spread spectrum (DSSS)** operating in the 2.4-GHz ISM band, at data rates of 1 Mbps and 2 Mbps.
- In the United States, the FCC (Federal Communications
- Commission) requires no licensing for the use of this band.

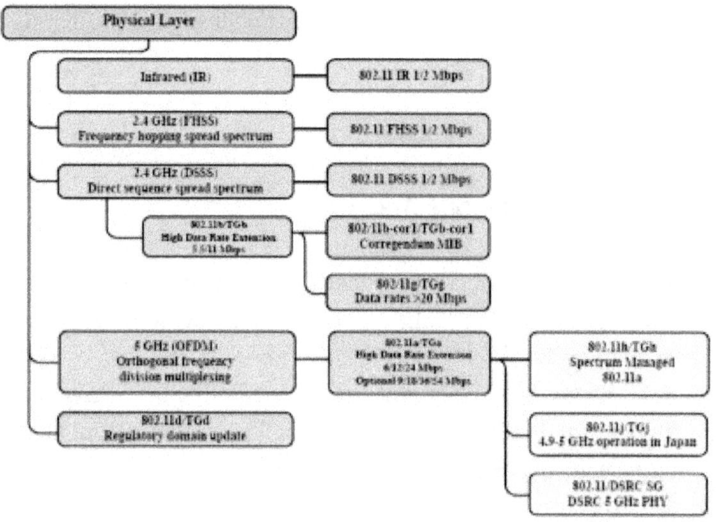

Figure 5: IEEE 802.11 physical layer

Standard	Band (GHz)	Bandwidth (MHz)	Modulation	Advanced Antenna Technology	Maximum data Rate
802.11	2.4	20	DSSS,FHSS	N/A	2 Mbps
802.11b	2.4	20	DSSS	N/A	11 Mbps
802.11a	2.4	20	OFDM	N/A	54 Mbps
802.11g	5	20	DSSS,OFDM	N/A	54 Mbps
802.11n	2.4	20,40	OFDM	MIMO up to four spatial streams	600 Mbps
802.11ad	60	60	SC,OFDM	Beamforming	7 Gbps
802.11ac	5	40,80,160	OFDM	MIMO, MU-MIMO, unto eight spatial streams	7 Gbps

- The number of channels available depends on the bandwidth allocated by the various national regulatory agencies.
- This ranges from 13 in most European countries to just one available channel in Japan.

- **Frequency-hopping spread spectrum (FHSS)** operating in the 2.4-GHz ISM band, at data rates of 1 Mbps and 2 Mbps.
- The number of channels available ranges from 23 in Japan to 70 in the United States.
- **Infrared** at 1 Mbps and 2 Mbps operating at a wavelength between 850 and 950nm.
-

Wi-Fi Protected Access

- The original 802.11 specification included a set of security features for privacy and authentication which, unfortunately, were quite weak.
- For privacy 802.11 defined the Wired Equivalent Privacy (WEP) algorithm. WEP makes use of the RC4 encryption algorithm using a 40-bit key.
- A later revision enables the use of a 104-bit key. For authentication, 802.11 requires that the two parties share a secret key not shared by any other party and defines a protocol by which this key can be used for mutual authentication.
- The privacy portion of the 802.11 standard contained major weaknesses. The 40-bit key is woefully inadequate.

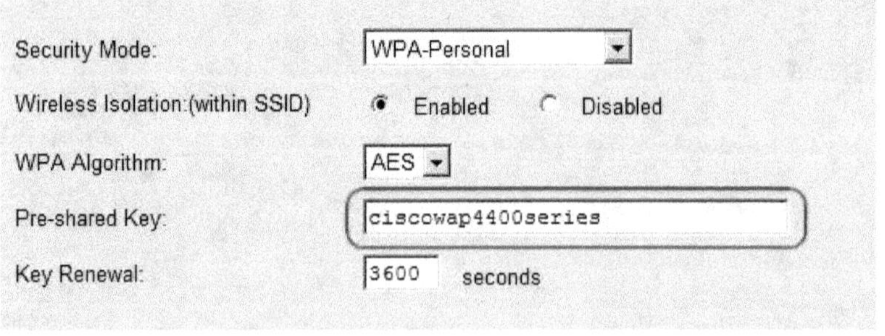

-

- Even the 104-bit key proved to be vulnerable, due to a variety of weaknesses both internal and external to the protocol supporting WEP.

- These vulnerabilities include the heavy reuse of keys, the ease of data access in a wireless network, and the lack of any key management within the protocol.

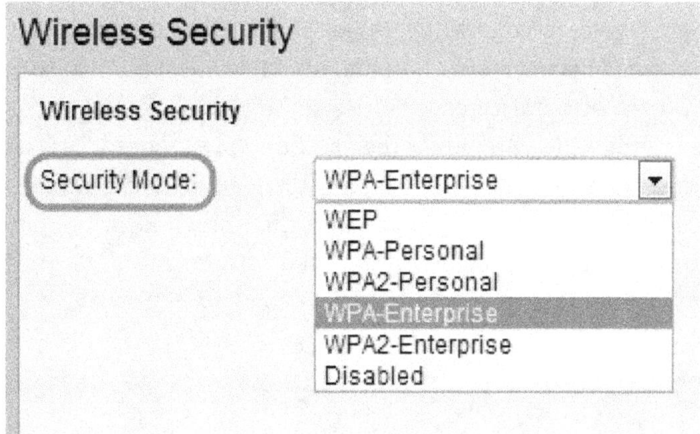

- The 802.11i task group has developed a set of capabilities to address the WLAN security issues.
- In order to accelerate the introduction of strong security into WLANs, the Wi-Fi Alliance promulgated **Wi-Fi Protected Access (WPA) as a Wi-Fi standard.**
- WPA is a set of security mechanisms that eliminates mos1 802.11 security issues and was based on the current state of the 802.11i standard.
- As 802.11i evolves, WPA will evolve to maintain compatibility. IEEE 802.11i addresses three main security areas: authentication, key management, and data transfer privacy. To improve authentication, 802.11i requires the use of an authentication server (AS) and defines a more robust authentication protocol.
- The AS also plays a role in key distribution. For privacy, 802.1li provides three different encryption schemes.

- The scheme that provides a long-term solution makes use of the Advanced Encryption Standard (AES) with 128-bit keys.
- However, because the use of AES would require expensive upgrades to existing equipment, alternative schemes based on 104-bit RC4 are also defined.
- Figure gives a general overview of 802.11i operation. First, an exchange between a station and an AP enables the two to agree on a set of security capabilities to be used. Then an exchange involving the AS and the station pro vides for secure authentication. The AS is responsible for key distribution to the A P, which in turn manages and distributes keys to stations. Finally, strong encryption is used to protect data transfer between the station and the AP.

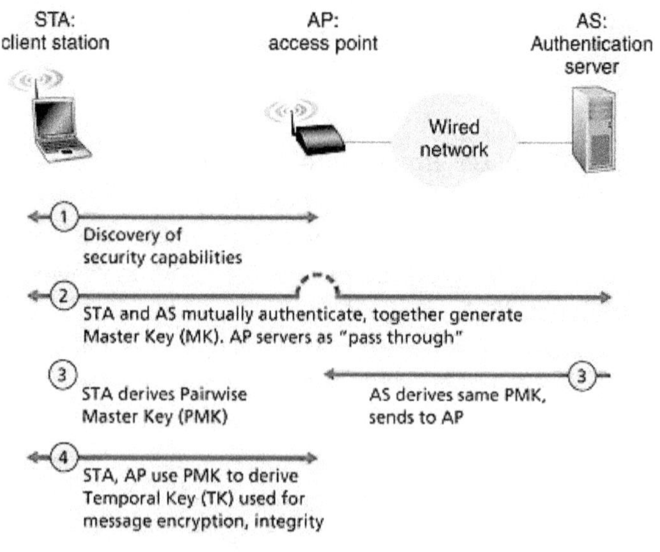

Figure 6: 802.11i Operational Phases

-

The 802.11i architecture consists of three main ingredients:

- **Authentication**: A protocol is used to define an exchange between a user and an AS that provides mutual authentication and generates temporary keys to be used between the client and the AP over the wireless link.
- **Access control**: This function enforces the use of the authentication function, routes the messages properly, and facilitates key exchange. It can work with a variety of authentication protocols.
- **Privacy with message integrity**: MAC-level data (E .g., an LLC PDU) are encrypted, along with a message integrity code that ensures that the data have not been altered.
-

Wireless LAN security issues OR What do you understand by hidden & exposed terminal problem in wireless LAN.

- IEEE 802.11 includes several security features:

  - Open system and shared key authentication modes
  - Service set identifiers-SSID
  - Wired Equivalent Privacy-WEP

- Security: A message transferred through wireless communication can be intercepted without physical access by any one.
- Any person, sitting in the vicinity of a WLAN with a transceiver with a capability to listen/talk, can pose a threat.
- Unfortunately, the same hardware or algorithms that are used for WLAN communication can be employed for such attacks. To make the WLANs reliable the following security goals were considered:

  - Confidentiality
  - Data Integrity
  - Access Control

- And following security measures are a part of the 802.11 IEEE protocol:

  - Authentication
  - Association
  - Encryption

- For communication purpose in wireless environment, the client should be authenticated person, and then only he or she may be able to associate with other client and the data that is to be transferred between two clients should be sent in encrypted form.
- In this problem, the transmission range of A reaches B but not C. Similarly, the range of C reaches B but not A. Also the range of B reaches both A and C.
- Now, the node A starts to send something to B and C, but C doesn't receive this transmission.
- Now C also wants to send data to B and senses the carrier. As it
- senses it to be free, it also starts sending to B.

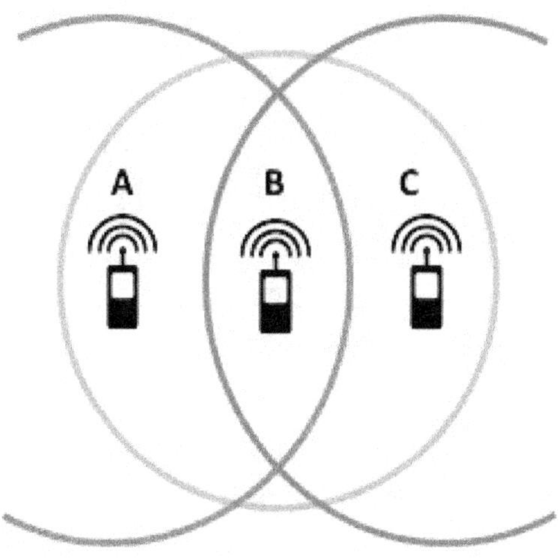

Figure 7: Hidden Terminal Problem Example

- A hidden terminal problem occurs when two nodes that are outside each other's range performs simultaneous transmission to a node that is within the range of each of them resulting in a collision.
- That means the data from both parties A and C will be lose during the collision.
- Hidden nodes mean increased probability of collision at the receiver end.
- One solution to avoid this is to have the channel sensing range much greater than the receiving range. Another solution is to use
- the Multiple Access with Collision Avoidance (MACA).

5

Bluetooth

Introduction of Bluetooth

- It was initiated in the year 1989 by Nils Rydbeck and "Bluetooth" name is taken from a 10th- century Danish king Harald Blåtand named Harald Bluetooth, who was said to unite disparate, warring regional factions. Like its namesake.
- Bluetooth technology brings together a broad range of devices across many different industries through a unifying communication standard.
- Bluetooth is a short-range wireless communication technology that allows devices such as mobile phones, computers, and peripherals to transmit data or voice wirelessly over a short distance.
- The purpose of Bluetooth is to replace the cables that normally connect devices, while still keeping the communications between them secure.
- Example, mobile, headset, laptop, camera, etc.

- Bluetooth allows users to make ad hoc wireless connections between devices like mobile phones, desktop or notebook computers wirelessly.
- Bluetooth operates in a globally available frequency bad ensuring interoperability. Bluetooth uses the unlicensed 2.4GHz ISM (Industrial Scientific and Medical) frequency band.

Piconet and Scatternet

- Bluetooth protocol uses the concept of master and slave relation.
- In a master-slave protocol a device cannot talk as and when they desire. They need to wait till the time the master allows them to talk.
- The master and slaves together form a **piconet**. Up to seven "slave" devices can be set to communicate with a "master". **(M:**

Master, S: Slave)

-
- There are 79 available Bluetooth channels spaced 1MHz apart from 2.402 GHz to 2.480 GHz.
- The Bluetooth standard is managed and maintained by Bluetooth Special Interest Group.
- Data transfer at a speed of about 720 Kbps within 50 meters (150 feet) of range or beyond through walls, clothing and even
- luggage bags.

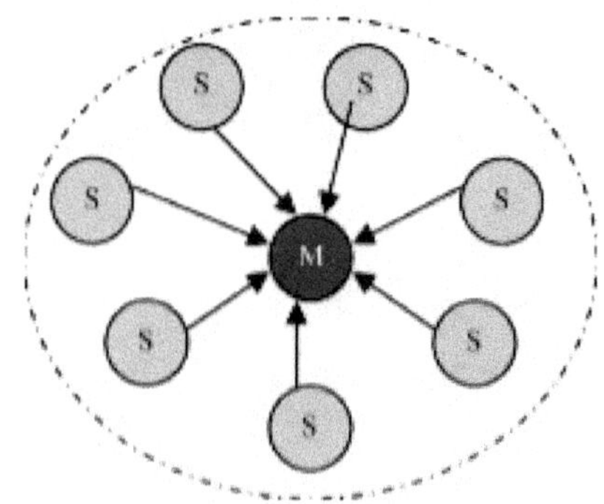

Figure 1: Master-Slave connection in Piconet

-
- Several of these piconets can be linked together to form a larger network in an ad-hoc manner.
- The topology can be thought as a flexible, multiple piconet structure. This network of piconets is called **Scatternet.**

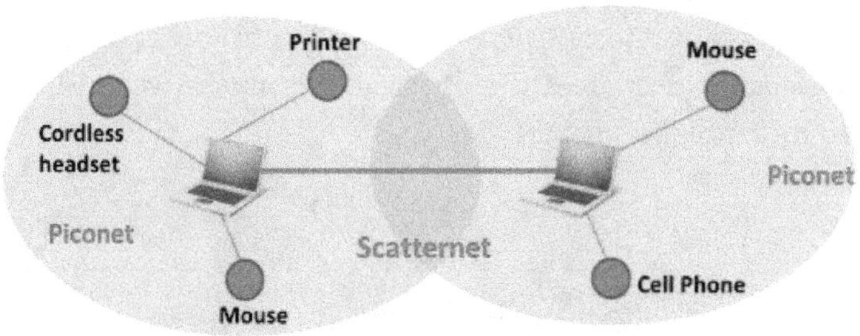

Figure 2: Piconet and Scatternet

- A Scatternet is formed when a device from one piconet also acts as a member of another piconet. In this scheme, a device being a master in one piconet can simultaneously be a slave in the other one.

Bluetooth Protocol Stack

- Bluetooth protocol stack can be thought of as a combination of multiple application specific stacks.
- Bluetooth uses spread spectrum technologies at the Physical Layer while using both direct sequence and frequency hopping spread spectrum technologies.
- It uses connectionless (ACL–Asynchronous Connectionless Link) and connection-oriented (SCO– Synchronous Connection-oriented Link) links.
- Bluetooth protocol stack can be divided into four basic layers according to their functions.

1. Bluetooth Core Protocols:

- This comprises of baseband, Link Manager Protocol (LMP), Logical Link Control and Adaption Protocol (L2CAP), and Service Discovery Protocol (SDP).
- **Baseband**: It enables the physical RF link between Bluetooth units forming a piconet.

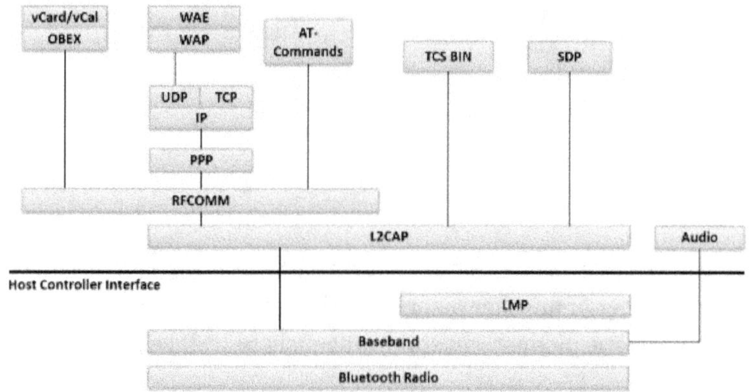

Figure 3: Bluetooth Protocol Stack

- This layer uses inquiry and paging procedures to synchronize the transmission with different Bluetooth devices. Using SCO and ACL link different packets can be multiplexed over the same.
- **Link Manager Protocol:** When two Bluetooth devices come within each other's range, link managers of either device discover each other.
- LMP then engages itself in peer-to-peer message exchange. These messages perform various security functions starting from authentication to encryption.
- It also controls the power modes, connection state, and duty cycles of Bluetooth devices in a piconet.

- **Logical Link Control and Adaption Protocol (L2CAP):** This layer is responsible for segmentation of large packets and the reassembly of fragmented packets.
- L2CAP is also responsible for multiplexing of Bluetooth packets from different applications.
- **Service Discovery Protocol (SDP):** It enables a Bluetooth device to join a piconet. Using SDP a device inquires what services are available in a piconet and how to access them.
- SDP uses a client-server model where the server has a list of services defined through service records.
- In Bluetooth device there is only one SDP server. If a device provides multiple services, one SDP server acts on behalf of all of them.

1. Cable Replacement Protocol:

- This protocol has only one member which is Radio Frequency Communication (RFCOMM).
- **RFCOMM:** It is a serial line communication protocol and is based on ETSI 07.10 specification.

- The "cable replacement" protocol emulates RS-232 control and data signals over Bluetooth Baseband Protocol.

1. Telephony Control Protocol:

- It comprises of two protocol stacks, viz., Telephony Control Specification Binary (TCS BIN), and the AT-commands.
- **Telephony Control Specification Binary (TCS BIN):** It is a bit-oriented protocol. It defines all the call control signaling protocol for set up of speech and data calls between Bluetooth devices.
- It also defines mobility management procedures for handling groups of Bluetooth TCS devices. It is based on the ITU-T Recommendation Q.931.

- **AT-Commands:** It defines a set of AT-commands by which a mobile phone can be used and controlled as a modem for fax and data transfers.
- AT commands are used from a computer or DTE to control a modem or DC. They are based on ITU-T Recommendation V.250 and GSM 07.07.

3. Adopted Protocols:

- This has many protocols stacks like Point-to-Point Protocol (PPP), TCP/IP Protocol, OBEX (Object Exchange Protocol), Wireless Application Protocol (WAP), vCard, vCalender, Infrared Mobile Communication (IrMC), etc.
- **PPP Bluetooth:** This offers PPP over RFCOMM to accomplish point-to-point connections. Point-to-Point Protocol is the means of taking IP packets to/from the PPP layer and placing them onto the LAN.
- **TCP/IP:** This protocol is used for communication across the Internet. TCP/IP stacks are used in numerous devices including printers, handheld computers, and mobile handsets.
- TCP/IP/PPP is used for the all Internet bridge usage scenarios.
- **OBEX Protocol:** OBEX is a session protocol developed by the Infrared Data Association (IrDA) to exchange objects.
- OBEX provides the functionality of HTTP in a much lighter fashion. It defines a folder listing object, which can be used to browse the contents of folders on remote devices.
- **Content Formats:** vCard and vCalender specifications define the format of an electronic business card and personal calendar entries developed by the Versit consortium.
- These content formats are used to exchange messages and notes. They are defined in the IrMC specification.

Bluetooth Security

- Bluetooth offers security infrastructure starting from authentication, key exchange to encryption.
- At lower levels of the protocol stack, Bluetooth uses the publicly available cipher algorithm known as SAFER+ to authenticate a device's identity.

Application of Bluetooth

Model	Description
File Transfer	Refers to object transfer or transfer of files between devices.
Internet Bridge	In this model, a cordless modem acts as a modem to a PC and provides dial-up networking and faxing facilities.
LAN Access	Multiple data terminals use a LAN access point (LAP) as a wireless connection to an Ethernet LAN.
Synchronization	The synchronization model enables a device-to-device synchronization of data.
Headset	It is wirelessly connected and can act as an audio input-output interface of remote devices.

1.

6

Android – Architecture & Application Framework

1. *Android – Architecture & Application Framework*

- Android operating system is a stack of software components which is roughly divided into five sections and four main layers as shown below in the architecture diagram.

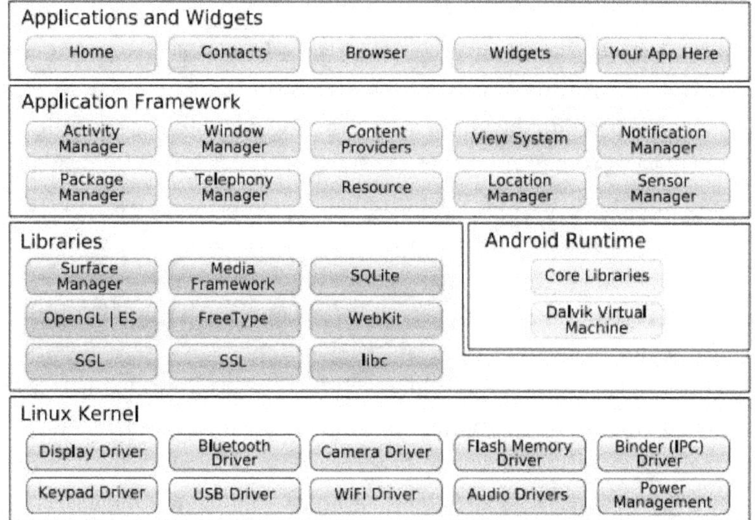

Linux kernel

- This provides a level of abstraction between the device hardware and it contains all the essential hardware drivers like camera, keypad, display etc.
- The kernel handles all the things that Linux is really good at such as networking and a vast array of device drivers, which take the pain out of interfacing to peripheral hardware.

Libraries

- On top of Linux kernel there is a set of libraries including open-source Web browser engine WebKit, well known library libc.
- SQLite database which is a useful repository for storage and sharing of application data, libraries to play and record audio and video, SSL libraries responsible for Internet security etc.

Android Libraries

- This category encompasses those Java-based libraries that are specific to Android development. Examples of libraries in this category include the application framework libraries in addition to those that facilitate user interface building, graphics drawing and database access. A summary of some key core Android libraries available to the Android developer is as follows.

- **android.app** – Provides access to the application model and is the cornerstone of all Android applications.
- **android.content** – Facilitates content access, publishing and messaging between applications and application components.
- **android.database** – Used to access data published by content providers and includes SQLite database management classes.
- **android.opengl** – A Java interface to the OpenGL ES 3D graphics rendering API.
- **android.os** – Provides applications with access to standard operating system services including messages, system services and inter-process communication.
- **android.text** – Used to render and manipulate text on a device display.
- **android.view** – The fundamental building blocks of application user interfaces.
- **android.widget** – A rich collection of pre-built user interface components such as buttons, labels, list views, layout managers, radio buttons etc.
- **android.webkit** – A set of classes intended to allow web-browsing capabilities to be built into applications.

Android Runtime

- This section provides a key component called Dalvik Virtual Machine which is a kind of Java Virtual Machine specially designed and optimized for Android.

- The Dalvik VM makes use of Linux core features like memory management and multi-threading, which is intrinsic in the Java language. The Dalvik VM enables every Android application to run in its own process, with its own instance of the Dalvik virtual machine.
- The Android runtime also provides a set of core libraries which enable Android application developers to write Android applications using standard Java programming language.

Application Framework

- The Application Framework layer provides many higher-level services to applications in the form of Java classes. Application developers are allowed to make use of these services in their applications.
- **Activity Manager** – Controls all aspects of the application lifecycle and activity stack.
- **Content Providers** – Allows applications to publish and share data with other applications.
- **Resource Manager** – Provides access to non-code embedded resources such as strings, color settings and user interface layouts.
- **Notifications Manager** – Allows applications to display alerts and notifications to the user.
- **View System** – an extensible set of views used to create application user interfaces.

Applications

- You will find all the Android application at the top layer. You will write your application to be installed on this layer only. Examples of such applications are Contacts Books, Browser, and Games etc.

Application Components

- Application components are the essential building blocks of an Android application. These components are loosely coupled by the application manifest file AndroidManifest.xml that describes each component of the application and how they interact.
- There are following four main components that can be used within an Android application

Activities

- An activity represents a single screen with a user interface; in-short Activity performs actions on the screen. For example, an email application might have one activity that shows a list of new emails, another activity to compose an email, and another activity for reading emails. If an application has more than one activity, then one of them should be marked as the activity that is presented when the application is launched.

```
public class MainActivity extends Activity {
}
```

Services

- A service is a component that runs in the background to perform long-running operations. For example, a service might play music in the background while the user is in a different application, or it might fetch data over the network without blocking user interaction with an activity.

```
public class MyService extends Service {
}
```

Broadcast Receivers

- Broadcast Receivers simply respond to broadcast messages from other applications or from the system. For example, applications can also initiate broadcasts to let other applications know that some data has been downloaded to the device and is available for them to use, so this is broadcast receiver who will intercept this communication and will initiate appropriate action.

- A broadcast receiver is implemented as a subclass of BroadcastReceiver class and each message is broadcaster as an Intent object.

```
public class MyReceiver extends BroadcastReceiver { public void onReceive(context,intent){
   }
}
```

Content Providers

- A content provider component supplies data from one application to others on request. Such requests are handled by the methods of the ContentResolver class. The data may be stored in the file system, the database or somewhere else entirely.
- A content provider is implemented as a subclass of ContentProvider class and must implement a standard set of APIs that enable other applications to perform transactions.

```
public class MyContentProvider extends ContentProvider {
public void onCreate(){
   }
}
```

1. *App Manifest File*

- Every application must have an AndroidManifest.xml file (with precisely that name) in its root directory. The manifest file provides essential information about your app to the Android system, which the system must have before it can run any of the app's code.

Manifest file structure

```xml
<?xml version="1.0" encoding="utf-8"?>
<manifest>
<uses-permission />
<permission />
<permission-tree />
<permission-group />
<uses-sdk />
<uses-configuration />
<uses-feature />
<supports-screens />
<compatible-screens />
<supports-gl-texture />
<application>
<activity>
<intent-filter>
<action />
<category />
<data />
</intent-filter>
<meta-data />
</activity>
<activity-alias>
<intent-filter> ... </intent-filter>
<meta-data />
</activity-alias>
<service>
<intent-filter> ... </intent-filter>
<meta-data/>
</service>
<receiver>
<intent-filter> ... </intent-filter>
<meta-data />
</receiver>
<uses-library />
</application>
```

</manifest>

<manifest>

<manifest   xmlns:android="http://schemas.android.com/apk/res/android" package="*string*"

android:versionCode="*integer*" android:versionName="*string*">

. . .

</manifest>

- The root element of the AndroidManifest.xml file. It must contain an <application> element and specify xmlns:android and package attributes.

<application   android:allowBackup=["true" | "false"] android:icon="*drawable   resource*" android:label="*string   resource*" android:logo="*drawable resource*" android:name="*string*">

. . .

</application>

- The declaration of the application. This element contains sub elements that declare each of the application's components and has attributes that can affect all the components.

<activity>

<activity android:icon="*drawable resource*" android:label="*string resource*" android:name="*string*" android:theme="*resource or theme*">

. . .

</activity>

- Declares an activity that implements part of the application's visual user interface. All activities must be represented by <activity> elements in the manifest file. Any that are not declared there will not be seen by the system and will never be run.

<action>

```
<action android:name="string" />
```

- Adds an action to an intent filter. An <intent-filter> element must contain one or more <action> elements. If it doesn't contain any, no Intent objects will get through the filter. See Intents and Intent Filters for details on intent filters and the role of action specifications within a filter.

```
<service>
<service android:icon="drawable resource" android:label="string resource" android:name="string" android:process="string" >
    . . .
</service>
```

- They're used to implement long-running background operations or a rich communications API that can be called by other applications.
- All services must be represented by <service> elements in the manifest file. Any that are not declared there will not be seen by the system and will never be run.

1. *Android Layouts*

- The basic building block for user interface is a View object which is created from the View class and occupies a rectangular area on the screen and is responsible for drawing and event handling. View is the base class for widgets, which are used to create interactive UI components like buttons, text fields, etc.
- The ViewGroup is a subclass of View and provides invisible container that hold other Views or other ViewGroups and define
- their layout properties.

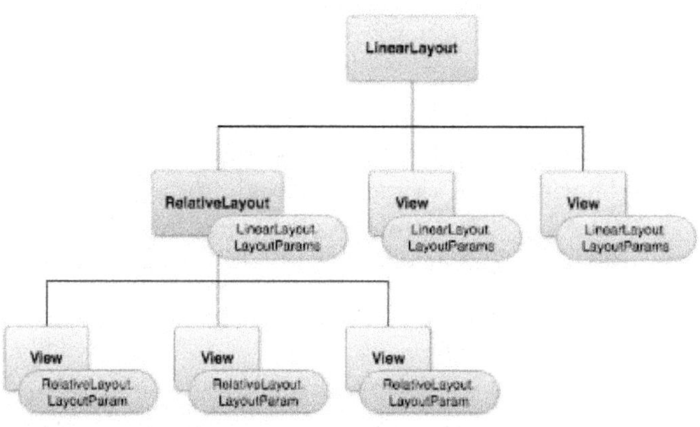

Linear Layout

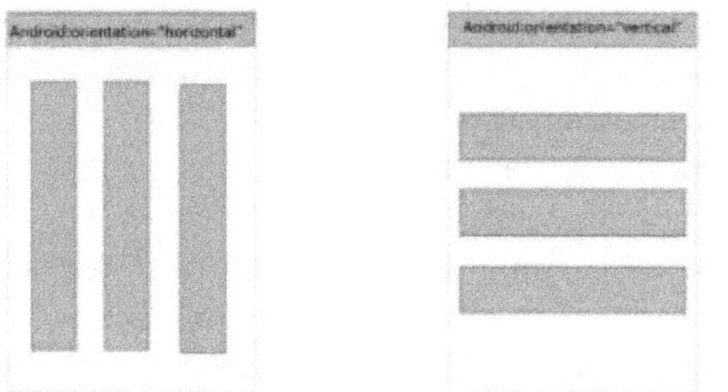

- A Layout that arranges its children in a single column or a single row.
- android:id
- This is the ID which uniquely identifies the layout.
- This specifies how an object should position its content, on both the X and Y axes. Possible values are top, bottom, left, right, center, center_vertical, center_horizontal etc.
- android:gravity

android:orientation

- This specifies the direction of arrangement and you will use "horizontal" for a row, "vertical" for a column. The default is horizontal.

```
<?xml version="1.0" encoding="utf-8"?>
<LinearLayout    xmlns:android="http://schemas.android.com/
apk/res/android" android:layout_width="match_parent"
    android:layout_height="             match_parent          "
android:orientation="vertical" >
    <Button                          android:id="@+id/btnA"
android:layout_width="match_parent"
android:layout_height="wrap_content" android:text="Button A"/>
    <Button                          android:id="@+id/btnB"
android:layout_width="match_parent"
android:layout_height="wrap_content" android:text="Button B"/>
</LinearLayout>
```

Relative Layout

- RelativeLayout is a view group that displays child views in relative positions. The position of each view can be specified as relative to sibling elements (such as to the left-of or below another view) or in positions relative to the parent RelativeLayout area (such as aligned to the bottom, left or center).
- android:layout_alignParentTop

  - If "true", makes the top edge of this view match the top edge of the parent.

- android:layout_centerVertical

  - If "true", centers this child vertically within its parent.
  - android:layout_below

- ◦ Positions the top edge of this view below the view specified with a resource ID.

- ◦ android:layout_toRightOf

- ◦ Positions the left edge of this view to the right of the view specified with a resource ID.

```
<?xml version="1.0" encoding="utf-8"?>
<RelativeLayout    xmlns:android="http://schemas.android.com/apk/res/android"
    android:layout_width="match_parent"
android:layout_height="match_parent">
    <Spinner
    android:id="@id/SpA"                android:layout_width="96dp"
android:layout_height="wrap_content"
android:layout_alignParentRight="true" />
    <Button
    android:layout_width="96dp"
android:layout_height="wrap_content"
android:layout_below="@id/SpA"
android:layout_alignParentRight="true"/>
    </RelativeLayout>
ScrollView
```

- **ScrollView** is a special kind of layout, designed to hold view larger than its actual size. When the Views size goes beyond the ScrollView size, it automatically adds scroll bars and can be scrolled vertically.
- ScrollView can hold only one direct child. This means that, if you have complex layout with more view controls, you must enclose them inside another standard layout like LinearLayout, TableLayout or RelativeLayout.
- You can specify layout_height and layout_width to adjust height and width of screen.

- Scrollview is ideal for screens where scrolling is required, but it is an overhead when scroll view is used to render a larger list of data. Android provides specialized adapter views like ListView, GridView are recommended for long lists.
- You should never use a ScrollView with a ListView or GridView, because they both takes care of their own vertical scrolling.
- ScrollView only supports vertical scrolling. Use HorizontalScrollView for horizontal scrolling.

```
<ScrollView  xmlns:android="http://schemas.android.com/apk/res/android"
    android:layout_width="match_parent"
android:layout_height="wrap_content"
android:orientation="vertical">
    <LinearLayout
    android:layout_width="match_parent"
android:layout_height="wrap_content"
android:orientation="vertical">
    <ImageView
    android:id="@+id/imageView"
android:layout_width="wrap_content"
android:layout_height="200dp"    android:scaleType="centerCrop"
android:src="@drawable/image" />
    <TextView
    android:id="@+id/textView"
android:layout_width="wrap_content"
android:layout_height="wrap_content"    android:text="@string/description"/>
    </LinearLayout>
    </ScrollView>
Table Layout
```

- Android TableLayout going to be arranged groups of views into rows and columns. You will use the <TableRow> element to build a row in the table. Each row has zero or more cells; each cell can hold one View object.

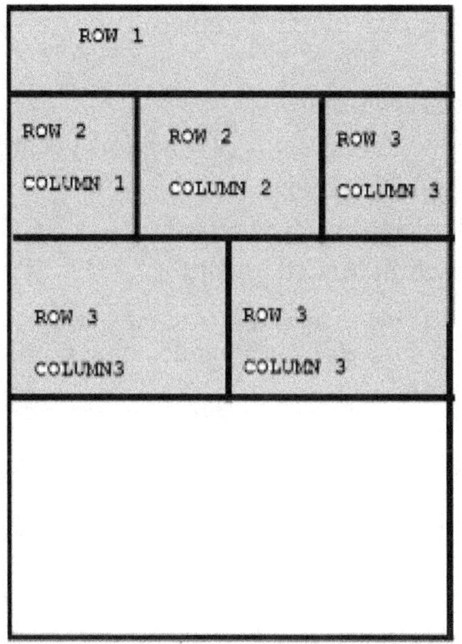

- android:collapseColumns

  - This specifies the zero-based index of the columns to collapse.

- android:collapseColumns

  - The zero-based index of the columns to shrink.

- android:stretchColumns

  - The zero-based index of the columns to stretch.

```
<TableLayout         xmlns:android="http://schemas.android.com/
apk/res/android"
   android:layout_width="match_parent"
android:layout_height="match_parent">

   . . .

   <!-- Row 2 with 3 columns -->
   <TableRow
   android:id="@+id/tableRow2"
android:layout_height="wrap_content"
android:layout_width="match_parent">
      <TextView
      android:id="@+id/TextView01" android:text="Row 2 column 1"
android:layout_weight="1"/>
      <TextView
      android:id="@+id/TextView02" android:text="Row 2 column 2"
android:layout_weight="1" />
      <TextView
      android:id="@+id/TextView03" android:text="Row 2 column 3"
android:layout_weight="1" />
   </TableRow>
   </TableLayout>
   FrameLayout
```

- Frame Layout is designed to block out an area on the screen to display a single item. Generally, FrameLayout should be used to hold a single child view, because it can be difficult to organize child views in a way that's scalable to different screen sizes without the children overlapping each other.
- android:foreground

  ◦ This defines the drawable to draw over the content and possible values may be a color value, in the form of "#rgb", "#argb", "#rrggbb", or "#aarrggbb".

- android:foregroundGravity

- ◦ Defines the gravity to apply to the foreground drawable. The gravity defaults to fill. Possible values are top, bottom, left, right, center, center_vertical, center_horizontal etc.

- android:measureAllChildren

  - ◦ Determines whether to measure all children or just those in the VISIBLE or INVISIBLE state when measuring. Defaults to false.

```
<FrameLayout    xmlns:android="http://schemas.android.com/apk/res/android"
    android:layout_width="match_parent"
android:layout_height="match_parent">
    <ImageView
    android:src="@drawable/ic_launcher"
android:scaleType="fitCenter"        android:layout_height="250px"
android:layout_width="250px"/>
    <TextView
    android:text="Frame                             Demo"
android:layout_height="wrap_parent"
android:layout_width="wrap_parent" android:gravity="center"/>
    </FrameLayout>
```

1. *How to download and Install android studio?*

- Following is the list of software's you will need before you start your Android application programming.
- Java JDK5 or later version
- Android Studio

Set-up Java Development Kit (JDK)

- You can download the latest version of Java JDK from Oracle's Java site – Java SE Downloads.

- http://www.oracle.com/technetwork/java/javase/downloads/index.html
- You will find instructions for installing JDK in downloaded files, follow the given instructions to install and configure the setup. Finally set PATH and JAVA_HOME environment variables to refer to the directory that contains java and javac, typically java_install_dir/bin and java_install_dir respectively.

Setup Android Studio

- Android Studio is the official IDE for android application development. It works based on IntelliJ IDEA; you can download the latest version of android studio from Android Studio 2.2 Download.
- https://developer.android.com/studio/index.html.
- If you are new to installing Android Studio on windows, you will find a file, which is named as android-studio-bundle-143.3101438-windows.exe.So just download and run on windows machine

Installation

- So let's launch Android Studio.exe, Make sure before launch Android Studio, Our Machine should require installed Java JDK.
- Once you launched Android Studio, it's time to mention JDK7 path or later version in android studio installer.
- Need to specify the location of local machine path for Android studio and Android SDK.
- Need to specify the ram space for Android emulator by default it would take 512MB of local machine RAM.
- At final stage, it would extract SDK packages into our local machine, it would take a while time to finish the task.
- After done all above steps perfectly, you must get finish button and it going to be open android studio project with Welcome to android studio message as shown below

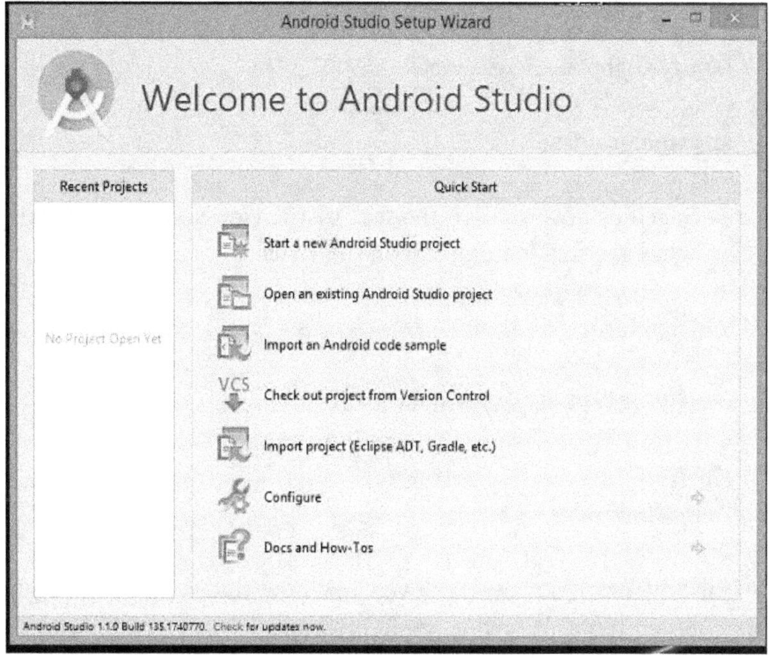

- You can start your application development by calling start a new android studio project. in a new installation frame should ask Application name, package information and location of the project.

1. *TextView, EditText View, Button View, RadioButton, CheckBox, ImageButton, RatingBar*

Textview
Definition

- A TextView displays text to the user and optionally allows them to edit it. A TextView is a complete text editor; however the basic class is configured to not allow editing.

Main Attributes of Text view:-

- **android:gravity**

  - Specifies how to align the text by the view's x- and/or y-axis when the text is smaller than the view.

- android:hint

  - Hint text to display when the text is empty.

EditText
Definition

- An EditText is an overlay over TextView that configures itself to be editable. It is the predefined subclass of TextView that includes rich editing capabilities.
- Edittext Attributes:-Following are the important attributes related to EditText control. You can check Android official documentation for complete list of attributes and related methods which you can use to change these attributes are run time.

- android:text

  - If set, specifies that this TextView has a textual input method and automatically corrects some common spelling errors.

- android:background

  - This is a drawable to use as the background.

- android:id

- ○ This supplies an identifier name for this view.

- **android:visibility**

  - ○ This controls the initial visibility of the view.

Button View
Definition

- A Button is a Push-button which can be pressed, or clicked, by the user to perform an action.

Button Attributes

- Following are the important attributes related to Button control. You can check Android official documentation for complete list of attributes and related methods which you can use to change these attributes are run time.
- android:drawableBottom

  - ○ This is the drawable to be drawn below the text.

- android:text
- This is the Text to display.
- android:background
- This is a drawable to use as the background.
- android:id

  - ○ This supplies an identifier name for this view.

- android:id

  - ○ This supplies an identifier name for this view.

Radio Buttton

- For Using Radio Button we use RadioGroup Control
- If we check one radio button that belongs to a radio group, it automatically unchecks any previously checked radio button within the same group.
- Radio Group Attributes
- Following are the important attributes related to RadioGroup control. You can check Android official documentation for complete list of attributes and related methods which you can use to change these attributes are run time.
- android:checkedButton

  - This is the id of child radio button that should be checked by default within this radio group.

- android:background

  - This is a drawable to use as the background.

- android:id

  - This supplies an identifier name for this view.

- android:visibility

  - This controls the initial visibility of the view.

- android:onClick

  - This is the name of the method in this View's context to invoke when the view is clicked.

- *CheckBox*
  Definition
- A CheckBox is an on/off switch that can be toggled by the user. You should use check-boxes when presenting users with a group

of selectable options that are not mutually exclusive.
- CheckBox Attributes
- Following are the important attributes related to CheckBox control. You can check Android official documentation for complete list of attributes and related methods which you can use to change these attributes are run time.Inherited from android.widget.TextView Class –
- android:autoText

  ◦ If set, specifies that this TextView has a textual input method and automatically corrects some common spelling errors.

- android:drawableRight

  ◦ This is the drawable to be drawn to the right of the text.

- android:text
- This is the Text to display. Inherited from android.view.View Class
- android:background

  ◦ This is a drawable to use as the background.

- android:contentDescription

  ◦ This defines text that briefly describes content of the view.

- android:id

  ◦ This supplies an identifier name for this view.

- android:onClick
- This is the name of the method in this View's context to invoke when the view is clicked.
- android:visibility

- ○ This controls the initial visibility of the view.

Image View
Definition

- An ImageButton is an AbsoluteLayout which enables you to specify the exact location of its children. This shows a button with an image (instead of text) that can be pressed or clicked by the user.

ImageButton Attributes

- Following are the important attributes related to ImageButton control. You can check Android official documentation for complete list of attributes and related methods which you can use to change these attributes are run time.
- Inherited from android.widget.ImageView Class
- android:adjustViewBounds

o Set this to true if you want the ImageView to adjust its bounds to preserve the aspect ratio of its drawable.

- android:baseline

  - ○ This is the offset of the baseline within this view.

- android:baselineAlignBottom

  - ○ If true, the image view will be baseline aligned with based on its bottom edge.

- android:cropToPadding

  - ○ If true, the image will be cropped to fit within its padding.

- android:src

  - This sets a drawable as the content of this ImageView.

- android:id

  - This supplies an identifier name for this vi

Rating Button
Definition

- Android RatingBar can be used to get the rating from the user. The Rating returns a floating- point number. It may be 2.0, 3.5, 4.0 etc.
- Android RatingBar displays the rating in stars. Android RatingBar is the subclass of AbsSeekBar class.
- The getRating() method of android RatingBar class returns the rating number.

Attributes:-

- android:id
- android:layout_alignParentTop
- android:layout_centerHorizontal
- android:layout_marginTop

Option Menu
Definition

- Android Option Menus are the primary menus of android. They can be used for settings, search, delete item etc.
- Here, we are going to see two examples of option menus. First, the simple option menus and second, options menus with images.

- Here, we are inflating the menu by calling the inflate() method of MenuInflater class. To perform event handling on menu items, you need to override onOptionsItemSelected() method of Activity class.

- We have to make another file in res/menu
- It contains three items as show below. It is created automatically inside the res/menu directory.

Author's Detail

Dr. Aditi Sharma
Associate Professor
Department of Computer Science and Engineering
Parul Institute of Technology,
Parul University, Vadodara, Gujarat
Mr. Himanshu Panadiwal
Assistant Professor
Department of Computer Science and Engineering
Parul Institute of Engineering and Technology
Parul University, Vadodara, Gujarat
Mr. Rahul Sharma
Assistant Professor
Department of Computer Science and Engineering
Parul Institute of Technology
Parul University, Vadodara, Gujarat
Mr. Rahul Anjana
Assistant Professor
Department of Computer Science and Engineering
Parul Institute of Technology,
Parul University, Vadodara, Gujarat